I0558281

Homeschooling

The Unexpected Path That Led Me to Homeschooling

(Reclaiming the Wonder in Your Child's Education, a New Way to Homeschool)

Robert Carlson

Published By **Elena Holly**

Robert Carlson

Homeschooling: The Unexpected Path That Led Me to Homeschooling (Reclaiming the Wonder in Your Child's Education, a New Way to Homeschool)

ISBN   978-1-998038-46-6

No part of this guidebook shall be reproduced in any form without permission in writing from the publisher except in the case of brief quotations embodied in critical articles or reviews.

Legal & Disclaimer

The information contained in this book is not designed to replace or take the place of any form of medicine or professional medical advice. The information in this book has been provided for educational & entertainment purposes only.

The information contained in this book has been compiled from sources deemed reliable, and it is accurate to the best of the Author's knowledge; however, the Author cannot guarantee its accuracy and validity and cannot be held liable for any errors or omissions. Changes are periodically made to this book. You must consult your doctor or get professional medical advice before using any of the suggested remedies, techniques, or information in this book.

Table Of Contents

Chapter 1: Why Homeschool

"A foolish faith in authority is the worst enemy of truth." Albert Einstein.

Traditional Schooling: What, Why, and How Schools Teach

We are all familiar with the hierarchical, one-size-fits all method of education that is prevalent in both the public and private schools we attend. An official curriculum is enforced by tests that are standardized in the hope of ensuring that the children are meeting standards. All children are taught exactly the same way in the same way, apart from gifted and talented and children with special needs. The gifted and talented programs typically accelerated versions of the curriculum that is provided by government. In some cases, special education could require that a child is present, tunes in to his iPod for the entire class and then gets a grade of D then moves onto the next level.

If you want to be fair to the educational system, think about the challenge of establishing the system of education for over fifty-three million students who are extremely diverse. They are from every kind of family that ranges from the extremely poor or homeless, to the most wealthy of people who have little or even no English to those who speak several languages. Certain children have not ventured beyond their neighborhood; while others are globe-trotters. A few families are run by hardworking parents or parents, others are headed are ruled by grandparents who have passed away or siblings, others by people suffering from mental or poverty disease, while others are run of them are ruled by criminals. Children will bring into the classroom the culture of their respective races as well as the regions of the nation. They will include the mechanical, the artistic as well as the intelligent and those who are athletic. There will be those who are unhappy, while others are emotional and mental, or perhaps drug addicts. Certain people are helpful, while others are equipped.

It attempts to achieve the equivalent of "herding cats" by adopting the same standards for all students. However, these standards vary from across states. With the variety I mentioned, it's a hard to believe that everything gets accomplished. Even in the most ideal situations, with the requirement to keep up to thirty or more kids engaged all day long in a classroom the schools often aren't able to find meaningful subjects to cover, but they still need to maintain in order. So, children learn a long listing of the capitals of each state and the ability division of negative fractions and a host of things just a handful of us can remember, or even find valuable in our own lives. The majority of institutions graduate students with high scores in many areas of academic knowledge but lacking in actual knowledge. In the eyes of most college students, it is now mandatory to obtain work doing all kinds of. Professors at colleges will inform that the majority of their early teaching is educational.

If you are content with the possibility that your child is attending a private school it could be that you're feeling an illusion of security. Many students who are disruptive at public schools are referred to private schools with the hope that they'll get straightened out. The kids who cause trouble often require additional school supervision or could remain disruptive and distracting other students from completing their coursework.

We'll take a look the words of John Taylor Gatto, schoolteacher for 30 years, ex- New York teacher of the year, as well as a world-class author and speaker has to say about the schools:

"My kids aren't sure what a mile means actually, but I'm sure they'll take a test. Similar to that it isn't clear about democracy, the meaning of money, the definition of an economy and what it is that can be fixed any issue. They've heard about Mogadishu as well as Saddam Hussein, but they could not give you which tree is that is in front of them if lives depended on it... There are some people can solve quadratic equations but aren't able to sew buttons on clothing or cook eggs; they could make answers bubble up using the number two pencil however, they aren't able to construct walls. Most of them have no notion that the majority of people on the planet are believers in God and how it can affect their way of do their daily lives.

"... The reality is that my children cannot plot their the future as they aren't aware of the place they're in or who they really are. Who do you think is who you are when you're not able to identify your personal family? How do you identify your family if no members have a regular time to be together? Who came up with this arrangement is a mystery, since surely this didn't happen by chance. happen."[7[7.

A lot of us have suggestions regarding how the schools could change, but this is not the subject of this article. Education is an enormous complex, enshrined, and complex bureaucracy. It is no wonder that the numerous attempts at improving the system have been met with huge protests. The majority of what's referred to as "reform" amounts to no anything more than tweaking the edges. Continuous testing mandated by the No Child Left Behind Act is not enough time for a creative teachers who want to motivate their pupils.

"The things that matter most should never be at the mercy of the things that matter least." Joseph Wolfgang of Goethe

Although it might seem that way that way, this post is not intended to be a school-bashing campaign. I truly believe that school administrators and teachers do their jobs very well, and of them are genuinely altruistic and idealistic. Some schools are able to be able to complete a satisfactory job in educating their pupils. However, is it the right location for your child to spend the majority of their time?

Do their peers at school have positive influences? Are your kids learning behaviours that don't align to your ideals? Are they receiving physical activities as well as the stimulation of the arts? Have these pursuits been neglected by a strict concentration on the academic? Do they have social interactions with other people from different cultures, ages or ethnicities? Is their socializing only limited to an exclusive group? Are they studying from real textbooks and people who've experienced reality? Do they have the real life skills? Are they repetitive learning, memorizing but then forgetting information rehashed from mind-numbing textbooks? Do their individual talents get recognized and further enhanced? Are they being taught to conform to molds?

" To be nobody but yourself in a world which is doing its best day and night to make you like everybody else, means to fight the hardest battle which any human being can fight and never stop fighting." -- e.e. Cummings

Socialization

One of the most common questions many people think of whenever the topic of homeschooling is "What about socialization?" This query seems to stem out of the somewhat bizarre notion that children can teach their peers the art of social interaction. How did this notion originate? For the majority of the history of humanity the children were surrounded through their family members. Their lives were spent in intimate contact with their siblings and parents as well as their grandparents, aunts cousins, uncles family members, friends as well as church members and professionals. Adults guided, corrected, and demonstrated how to conduct themselves in various occasions with individuals with different genders, ages or affiliations to church or parties qualifications, as well as occupations. Kids also learnt from farm animals and their patterns of social interaction. They witnessed births and deaths.

The children ate, slept reading, played, and performed the real job that was appreciated by their families and communities They also learned the importance working in a team. Adults were always around to help answer any questions or demonstrate the children how to accomplish something such as bake a pie, assist to harvest the crops, sew something, or even to read. This is the kind of child who feel a sense of their own worth that is based on actual demonstrations of skill and are aware that their interests must be put on the place of real-life issues.

We've been conditioned to believe that children should be removed from that multi-faceted environment and kept away from their surroundings in a space with 30 other children as well as a teacher or two for them to develop good behaviour. Anyone who has had any experience in a class will affirm that.

Kids and parents can assist each other in identifying birds based on their appearance or flight patterns, as well as by their behavior.

Sometimes parents feel that their children are supposed to be with (fewer and more) peers and they believe that schools can solve the problem? Friendship can be a challenging aspect to assess on behalf of someone else. In some cases, a child who has one close friend is taught much more about friends than one who has many friends. Certain children are attracted to the variety. Children who are shy may would rather have a more raunchy companion and conversely. Whatever the case, using an established home parents are able to adjust to the changing demands of children's social lives.

There is a chance that you will be shocked by the fact that parents and me can frequently determine how long a child was in school prior to becoming part of our homeschooling family. It is evident in the number of antisocial behaviors that he or she exhibits, such as bullying or teasing others, early sexuality, profanity or alcohol consumption, social clout and a prejudice toward individuals based on their race, gender or skin color, clothing and weight. or even glasses. The kids seem to take advantage of every distinction as a reason to be ostracized and tortured. We've all experienced the devastating consequences from these actions in numerous tragedies.

We have observed that the positive and uplifting environment inside our school quickly cools down any bad behaviour that previously students in school bring to it. It is my guess that this may be the way it occurs in other homeschooling groups also.

Professor. Raymond Moore, former principal, teacher, as well as superintendent for California public schools, wrote about his research-

Chapter 2: Academics

Apart from the necessity in teaching important, positive social abilities in the early between ten and twelve years old There are other compelling reasons to delay the time before presenting academic resources for your kids.

Child development specialists have long noted that children are not mentally or physically capable of formal education earlier than the age of ten. Jean Piaget (1896-1980) [9was among the earliest researchers in the subject, and discovered that certain stages that were appropriate for the successful completion of all types of learning. The idea of requiring children to study in which they weren't prepared is a recipe for failure, or behavioral problems. Abstract thinking, as he discovered is a process that begins at the age of 12.

Parents are often struck by the excitement of children in the initial couple of grades, and also the enthusiasm kids display in naming the letters and numbers. The majority of them say that they enjoy the school. Third graders too, if I asked how they enjoyed school, will say yes. However, by middle school only a handful of children said they liked school. at this point, I'm most likely to be receiving a request from the parents of schoolchildren who are suffering. If we observe the issues related to school increasing throughout the years, surely we should question the need to start early in school as well as the stress it causes.

An inconsistency between development levels and requirements for schooling is the primary reason for this in particular in the boys. Most likely, they will be labelled as having behavior issues and diagnosed as having a particular form of hyperactivity or attention deficit. Girls may also suffer from attention disorders however they're less likely to get diagnosed due to the fact that they're less readily recognized[10[10, 11]. They aren't prepared to be seated in front of a computer for prolonged durations of time. They are not able to speak or move around in a whim. Solution to this dilemma at school could involve using bribery (rewards) as well as discipline (punishment) and drugs or the separation of classes from others who have similar or even different issues within the class.

The majority of homeschoolers know or have heard tales of families that have had issues that disappeared after the child stopped in the school. Lanet Abrigo's essay (see Chapter 1 Parents in their own Words) is an example of this account.

Alternative schools, including Montessori and Waldorf have done a good job of teaching children appropriate knowledge and motor skills, but they frequently must resist the demands by parents to get children into with the basics of academics in their early years. The schools are also trying to teach social skills and positive values and improve the character of pupils. Their success is because of their small classes that is what makes them closer to families than schools. However, their curriculum could not be a great choice for your child in any particular moment, and instructors will need to develop strategies to encourage students to follow the rules to be expected, and also stop from engaging in activities they would rather do.

In the home, we are able to adapt the curriculum for the child and eliminate any need for bribes, or sanctions. The goal is to show that education is valuable just for the sake of it learning is an enjoyable thing to acquire as well as that we like learning about things that we're interested in. Kids can be taught to tackle issues that are significant to their lives. They can be taught a enthusiasm for learning through being attentive to their needs and the needs of their time.

It is also important to consider whether children are able to replicate the advice of their parents on the importance of schools and the fact that they are vital to achieve success. Our son was taught by third graders it would be impossible to find an employment if he did not attend schools. Students in third grade worried about having work? What happened to childhood?

I always told Thumper that it was likely an accurate statement. He probably wouldn't "get a job" if you didn't attend college. What he could be able to do was pursue a career or a passion which has now turned into a successful businessman. The job he was offered was temporary in the past where he was assisting with the preparation of the facility at Camp Woodward before camp started. He left that impression with an admiration for the amount of work those who have jobs are and the amount they are pay. He was also grateful for not having to be working a 9-to-5 job, instead he had made his own lucrative business as a videographer who freelances.

In the academics of secondary and high school years studying the subject matter that are part of a normal curriculum can be done quicker and more easily in the comfort of your home, without the hassles of chaotic students. Children who are older will have plenty of time to study these subjects while having time for a deeper dive into subjects and the things they're passionate about. The majority of them are well-prepared for the early college entry.

I Never Set Out to Be a Homeschooler!

I'm a student of the public schools system. I'm sure that you, as a readers, are. I've never considered an alternative option to receive an education. I received good grades in the time that it was considered something, and then was able to graduate from an elite university with a high mark.

Following graduation I had to face reality and accountable for major life decisions. In the educational system the path I took was simple: read the chapter ahead and answer the question at the end of each chapter, write the term paper, complete the next class, and begin with the next class. Then I began to wonder what the point of all this and was feeling like I'd missed some crucial lesson. However, I didn't think to question conventional educational concepts. Later, many years later that I realized how all of my education was relevant to my everyday life, nor could it be used to lead an authentic life.

The next 20 years giving, teaching counsel to individuals as well as writing, drawing watercolors as well as learning about the importance of fitness and nutrition, natural and political issues, and everything else that I found fascinating and helpful. I got married and met my partner, and together we determined that it was the right time to have our first child.

At that point we learned about courses offered by the Institutes for the Development of Human Potential located in Philadelphia named "How to increase your baby's Intelligence."[12The entire curriculum of the Institutes seemed impressive, and which is why we took a flight to attend the course of one week at their stunning premises. We didn't think the whole thing through however, it seemed to make sense to have our children emotionally, physically mentally, and physically better by intensive instruction beginning from the time of birth. The child would not have to take classes in the beginning, attend the Ivy League college in his teenage years, and then have a the most successful professional career possible in an admired area of study like the law or medicine. We went home from Philadelphia filled with ideas material, materials, and big expectations.

When the son of our family, Thumper who was born I joined the course. In the initial six to eight months, it worked very well. Through flashcards, I had taught his ability to distinguish all kinds of vocabulary, from words and phrases to bugs and presidents. Through the program's exercises, I noticed his vision, hearing as well as motor skills becoming superior in his current age. He began to let me know that, despite my enthusiasm for my presentations but he no longer interested in the information I learned was useful. The information may have been useful to some kids, but this was not the case the case for our son.

The first glimpse of doubt over the course at first, so I decided to drop some of the academic aspects. In the end, I realized that if I were curious about Thumper the program, I would easily find out his requirements in any moment. Thumper became my most trusted instructor.

By enforcing a few childproofing measures and a bit of childproofing, he could take in the world around him and comprehend it, without being shackled or needing to force it. He was fascinated by the sea which is why we went to the beach almost everyday. He was always looking for new things to discover. garden, the house shops, the TV and the kitchen. He also enjoyed painting instruments, dirt becoming a wonderful learning experience.

We've always been interested in the possibilities, however now we could do it without fear or remorse for the things we ought to be doing. It was a lot of enjoyable learning about new subjects as we grew close as a group.

At the time Thumper reached the age of three, others we had known left for preschool and the caretakers returned to their jobs. The idea didn't seem to make sense for me to take him off and so I set up the playgroup in order to have kids and adults to be with. A lot of the people who attended were our long-term friends.

Children who went to preschool had better skills at writing numbers or letters, and other such there was no child as curious, more eager to be learning as well as more enthusiastic and more enjoyable to spend time with like our boy. There aren't any more happy parents in the world.

What happened when the time came for classes? Through my 17 years of learning, I'd been exposed to the school model that was factory-based which had its top-down educational system, and it was also endorsed by the students in Philadelphia. This was the model I had planned to keep in perpetuity. However, by this point I'd began to think I was being too preposterous in thinking that an official from any government institution, or me, for that matter- would know what pieces of information could help the individual in 20 or more years from now in a world that was rapidly changing. I was certain that I needed to think about this seriously.

I approached this subject using the mind of a beginner, as which is described in the work of Zen Masters Shunryu Suzuki "The mind of a beginner is uncluttered, free from the typical habits of the professional and open to question, and be willing to explore all possibilities. This is the type of mind that can perceive things the way they are and step-by-step and quickly recognize the true essence of everything."[1313

To better inform myself about the choices we made in those years I read a lot of magazines and books. Additionally, I was observing our son, the other children and families. I was able to examine my upbringing and beliefs and questioned the beliefs I was and was surrounded by during my education and childhood.

Child development experts recommend delay in schooling until the age of 8 or 9, when children's bodies and minds are better prepared to tackle the academic material. This seemed to make sense to me. Especially as I viewed my energetic, boisterous son. It was clear that he'd be put to sleep with the traditional desk-and-pencil-learning that is common at schools.

We understood that many schools that are based on these discoveries, like Waldorf as well as Montessori were derived from the findings of research on childhood development phases and the needs. Although these programs work for a lot of children, once we were given an Waldorf Kindergarten curriculum and later, we noticed that we strayed from the curriculum more often instead of following the guidelines. The programs that have been developed for progressive learning are not without a dogma, and could not meet the needs of a specific child in any particular moment.

As time passed as we grew older, we became more confident in the system of inquiry-driven learning, also called "unschooling." I actually prefer the term "learning without schooling," because it reflects the idea that learning happens throughout the day, not only in the confines of the classroom. Actually, there is more learning happening within a shorter period of time, without the need for having to attend school because the pupil is motivated by their own interests and is not focused on the behavior of the other kids who challenge the system, or the craziness which the system employs to distract children long a day.

The delay in school due to Thumper was a sign that we needed an additional group of peers to talk to as the majority of kids had gone to school, as well as their parents worked. We started a family-oriented support group, called HAPPY (Homeschool adventures: A program for Parents and Children).

I planned weekly events that ranged from making crafts taking camping trips and whale-watch cruises, to excursion trips to the emergency fire department in the airport. We also had a dry cleaning shop as well as a ballet school, the solar observatory on top of Haleakala Volcano, and uncountable additional interesting locations. There were times when we had over fifty people involved in the event. Our community-based projects which included cleaning up the trash or caroling seniors with disabilities and creating crafts to help the women's shelter as well as our military personnel. The home we lived in was known by the name of "Hotel Nagasako," because there were always kids, homeschooled or conventionally educated, who were staying at our home.

Studying coastal geology for understanding the ways seismic activity affects our planet

I was able to use a handful of study guides in my early years I was a little rusty, but they were able to find an appropriate place to be used while I was working. They were an ingenuous way of learning that they only captivated Thumper only for a short period during the beginning period. The way we lived our lives naturally led us to meaningful lessons. We discovered our surroundings as we read books on subjects that we liked and interacted with a myriad of interesting individuals of different of ages. My husband had started his own firm and was working to supply our family with everything they needed and allow me to remain in the home with my child.

Thumper's birthdays, ages 8 and 9, have passed We were not quite ready to give Thumper to a day in a class filled with 30 kids of the same age as him and two adults. There was the entire world for him to explore and grow. We were able to see how kids in school behaved. We didn't want any of it.

As our family, we always put our feet on top of one another, working to make our lives enriching and fulfilling. We were able to learn U.S. geography from airplane windows while traveling. At the time of writing, Thumper has been to fifteen states, in the District of Columbia and to Canada, England, Germany, Italy, and France. Although he's seen images of the Vatican and the Sistine Chapel, and the Berlin Wall before, he's even been in the area. It was him who guided us through the Louvre in search of the most renowned artworks.

We've been blessed that we have been able to provide the opportunities that we have, however I do not want to give an impression that you have be able to travel far to get knowledge. It has been awe-inspiring by how many educated students know very little about their community, their local economics and politics as well as the plants they eat, the meals they consume, conditions, and the sky over their heads.

We've seen meteor showers on TV and attended adult astronomy courses. We've scoured to find Indian fossils from Michigan and old bottles in Hawaii. We've discovered the world around us as well as our own history and geography. Thumper developed his writing abilities not through drills or school essay, but through writing numerous letters to his parents as well as resumes for sponsors and video scripts and websites. In all of this, he followed his love of skating, skating in line, and developed his technology, including video editing in order to make video of himself and other athletes skating.

He took a full day excursion to an intermediate institution when he was 13 to determine if he would like to continue to attend schools. After the experience with the conviction to go on to homeschool. The details of the day as well as his thoughts about it can be found in the chapter 3.

We may have been as awestruck like everyone else when he reached 16 but had not been to school. We scheduled another visit that time around the high school in town, which he then decided to take it on and was enrolled as the junior. He attended for three terms and got all As and one failing grade, and then was forced to leave due to sheer discontent and boredom after spending long hours in the classroom and not getting much done. Then he got his GED that uses students who have graduated from high school as a control group, so the GED score is used to determine an indicator of his education colleagues across the country. 15 points put him within the top 13 percent of all students and the top 1% for the subject of literature. He's taken courses at the community college local to him as well as in the University of Hawaii, getting an identical GPA to the high school he attended.

Thumper has turned twenty-eight years old and is putting his videography and editing talents into an exciting career as a professional event videographer. For his job the name he uses is his official name of Jordan. Jordan is also an experienced professional in-line vert[16] skater. He been awarded his first ASA World Amateur Championship in 2002. The year he started his career with the top spot in American 4th globally. He's ranked among the top 10 worldwide every time since, which includes in the X Games and Gravity Games. He's got a strong base and wings, as well as a thriving profession, and is just the same kind of honorable and conscientious like any other person I have met. He is a prolific writer and reader as well as advertising a skate video and the sole proprietor of an event videography company.

Chapter 3: Children and Young Adults in Their Own Words

I questioned a small group of students about their opinions on the idea of homeschooling. The majority of them didn't have any clue as to what their peers were writing about. There are certain themes that appear throughout all reviews, but the specifics of what and how they did in school vary. A few went to school for only for a short time, others for a longer period of time, others were not even in school. Many have gone to college, and one has graduated with multiple qualifications. A school-educated child I have met who has written her tale to me with no being prompted.

The following is from Nani Jenson, who was a homeschooler who is now at the San Diego college:

While I am at the ceremony for my graduation from high school as I look at my class of graduates I am aware that everyone of us are thrilled to graduate. It's not as a result of being able show our worth to this world but the fact that we have been released from the shackles of high the school system. In a place where they praise clones instead of free thinking, I'm wondering what I did to get through the entire four years.

My homeschooling experience lasted until the fourth grade. at that point, I was able to see the reality of what being a kid involves, as I listened to my body's signal that I was starving or required to go to the bathroom and not having the bell of an authority figure. I was able to discover the things that others only watched on "informative" videos, and more importantly, I was able to break free and start my journey to become who I am today.

The school I attended has taught me a lot of things about the world, but most importantly, I learned from watching other students and what the role of the school, and rather than from the teachings in themselves. I was taught how to delay and fail to complete a number of days, yet still earn an 4.2 GPA. I was taught how to defend myself in front of my peers but without straying from the norm. In the end, I realized that people who never experienced childhood were considered to be the youngest students in my class.

The purpose of life is to be lived. Although I am not unhappy with my choice to go to the school system, I will forever be grateful to my parents who gave me a childhood not available to children who are educated in the early years.

Wendy is a friend to Nani She is currently a in senior year in UCSD. Wendy was a homeschooler throughout high school. She is married and is the mother of three-year-old.

A child who would like that she was homeschooled, and is a top performer in a private school

Art class is offered every Tuesday, for one hour. We were today studying Georgia O'Keeffe. We also took a faux flower - we do this each year - and we drew it using pastels. the design. The day wasn't particularly enjoyable since I thought I had finished, as I colored everything in and loved the result. Then I decided to my art teacher and showed her my artwork. After that, she said I was moving too fast and that I should reduce my speed. What's the purpose of being slow when you could speed up, as I do and remain extremely good? Then she forced me to change lots! At the point she stated she was happy but I was not happy! It's so annoying! It's my opinion that we need an art instructor who allows us know when this is the most effective thing we could accomplish and when we love the result. It's really irritating.

A blog by Lili Story, a teenager She writes on "What homeschooling means to me."

(Update The student has just earned an AA degree, with an overall 3.95 GPA and will be presented with "The President's Medal for Scholarly Excellence" by the college's president.)

The freedom of homeschooling allows me to be independent and the opportunity to become an unique person. When I'm at home, I have the opportunity to explore my interests, and the ways of living that are unique to me. I've managed to stay close to my family members, which is extremely crucial to me.

Since my schedule is open to change, I started my own business during summer, and integrated them into my studies. I've gained practical experiences in many actual-world skills that I likely wouldn't have.

The most memorable aspects of my life is my involvement in an amazing outdoor youth group, in which I've grown enormously. I'm in the third year of the program and it's completely changed my life. The program also covers a lot of the things I enjoy doing, such as hiking in the woods, studying plants and animals in the wild. My other hobbies include piano playing gardening, making food, creating, knitting, roller-skating and dancing, cooking as well as many other things!

Last but not least since I have homeschooled, I've cultivated my love of studying and my natural curiosity. I think this is essential to achieving every kind of success, and living life to the highest degree.

The sister of Lili, Rio Story, age nine:

The fact that I was homeschooled has altered my outlook on what my life might be. It's still schoolwork Of course however, I am having had so much pleasure. This week, I wore my tool belt, and was high up onto the roof of the home we're creating. I've done a lot of other tasks like installing concrete as well as cutting rebar and horse cantering, as well as working on the farm.

The life of a homeschooler is wonderful.

Chapter 4: What The Experts Suggest

As a parent of a sharp little wiggly child you're already aware of certain of these ideas. But, I'll make the list below to ensure that everything is available in one location for reference at a later time.

If you are teaching children who can be easy to distract, it is recommended to:

* Avoid sitting in a distracting location. It may sound obvious, however, your table at the kitchen might not be the most appropriate place to learn. Family members who are visiting to eat or enjoy the views from the windows is a major distraction for the child suffering from ADHD. With ADHD the problem is not that they aren't able to focus, but they struggle with to decide what they want to focus on or focusing on things that occur close by (especially that involve motion or sound from my personal experience) could divert their focus from work. You may not even

be aware that they've been distracted because of their poor timing you can tell that they are unable to be able to finish their work! Try to find an area that's low in distractions. In my case, for example, when our son was just learning to read the alphabet, he would build an fort in our living room. He would read in my ear from within it.

• Make your lessons interesting and fun, eerie, or unforgettable. or anything else you imagine! The addition of a hook, for example an adventure, joke or scavenger hunt can keep the kids engaged in the game, so that they'll be able to learn and not get bored.

• Use a variety of teaching methods. This can be a second "duh" point for many of you. It can, however, be harder to implement in practice since most curriculums have repetitive tasks. If you decide (or are choosing for your) the program that is consistent with exercises, for example "read this text, answer these questions" then you'll require a change in the exercises to ensure your child stays engaged with it. The following suggestions will help you accomplish this, as well as curriculums that include different activities later in this post.

• Include the interests of your child. If your child is a baseball fan take baseball tales and stats in your lesson plans. If they are interested in dinosaurs make writing and reading tasks around them. If you are able to take advantage of an existing focus point that you can draw greater focus on the subject and not be distracted by other activities going on.

Get active. Exercise can provide an immediate boost to concentration, therefore 15 or 20 minutes of activity prior to beginning classes can help you to improve your concentration in the initial few actions throughout your day. There is a possibility of adding a second exercise session in the afternoon, especially if there are other activities that you'd like to finish during the day. The addition of physical activity to lessons will help to get rid of some extra energy, and help them be focused at the content I've seen a couple of youngsters learn their times tables while on a trampoline and I have a child who is still averse to reading upside-down.

• Use games to improve concentration. Concentration is an ability that can be developed through practice even though children may be unable to master it. It is important to incorporate some practice in focus by playing games that are active, such as "Simon Says", "Red Light Green Light", and other quiet games like "Clue", chess, crossword puzzles, spot-the different puzzles and "Memory" can help improve abilities in the course of time.

Computer-based games specifically designed to increase concentration, like Lumosity.

• Spend time in the in the outdoors. The outdoors can be calming to most people. The exercise can be particularly useful for children who have been struggling. If you are able to take a break in the park every day or play a few games at your backyard, you'll burn off the energy as well as help break up your day.

Chapter 5: Education techniques

There are many different types of education and it's important to determine the type of education which is most suitable for your kids. It could be that the fashion is more important than changing the style of education in order to keep it engaging. When you've decided on a particular style, you may want to purchase programs that incorporate it or you can continue to use your existing program, adding the activities that make it interactive, engaging and exciting.

Hands-on:

The hands-on approach also increases your children's involvement with the content regardless of what it is in order to make sure your kids comprehend the subject better. Consider the differences when you talk about dividing cookies among groups of people vs. actually having cookie (or blocks) which you divide into families groups. Interacting with blocks can make division lessons enjoyable, interesting, and beneficial immediately.

The majority of people remember the activities faster, too, because they use multiple senses in order for performing. Sometimes it may appear taking longer accomplish - and occasionally it does - but the amount of comprehension will be more advanced.

Verbal:

A few kids, specifically kids who struggle with handwriting are benefited by doing a little exercises in a conversational manner. As an example, math questions tend to be solved by ear. Discussions on books or other books can be conducted in a conversational manner, while students are able to respond verbally to discussion questions that are included in the text instead of making notes of their answers.

Another alternative is to use Dragon (voice recognition program) for writing responses. It requires some training to master - mostly due to the fact that you must verbally use punctuation marks, for example "period" or "comma" however once you've got it set up, it will eliminate the tedious task of writing down details and permit the learner to follow the flow of speaking, not the writing. When the document has been completed, you are able to use the same editing procedure the way you normally would.

Story-based:

The new concepts can be taught by using narratives instead of textbooks. Literature can be used exclusively in the teaching of concepts or to use as an addition to the already existing courses. Some examples might be:

* Reading the "Sir Cumference" book relating to the math concept you're studying.

* Reading "Sassafras Science" books (http://sassafrasscience.com/) rather than a science textbook, and reinforce it using the activities in their activity guides.

* Utilizing "Fix-it" books from the Institute for Excellent in Writing (http://iew.com/fix) to improve handwriting and grammar. In this method, the student writes a portion of the story every day and is able to correct the grammar while they are doing it.

Read biographies about celebrities, or tales that are set in the past. A few examples be "Archimedes and the Door of Science" composed by Jeanne Bendick, or "George Washington and the General's

Dog" (part of the Step Into Reading series) written by Frank Murphy and Richard Walz.

Historical books that are that are written in narrative form is a great way for a deeper understanding of history instead of textbooks. Some good book lists can be found within the curriculum descriptions for Sonlight (http://www.sonlight.com/), Beautiful Feet (http://bfbooks.com/), and Build Your Library (http://buildyourlibrary.com/).

Learner methods

The concept of learning styles states that learning happens via different channels and senses that kinesthetic learners use learning through doing. visual learners like to get knowledge through their eyes. auditory learners are more likely to get information via their ears tactile learners would prefer learning by using their hands.

However, everybody has a different way of learning, we utilize all three (except for deafness or blindness) however, in different levels.

It is possible that you already have an idea of your child's preferred approach. If not, there are numerous quizzes online for you to determine and you can also use to read the guidebook "Discover Your Child's Learning Style" written by Mariaemma Wills that provides instructions for completing the complete learning profile to help your child.

It is important to integrate elements from every style into your lessons in order to determine how it works, and to aid to vary your lessons.

The Kinesthetics: integrate movements into your activities as often as is possible. Make math-related problems on the trampoline, make diagrams on the sidewalk using chalk, act out a story that you have read, take an exercise through the city while you discuss your literature assignments, or go on outings.

Visual: Include images or sample material whenever you can. Utilize different fonts and colors to print your work. Learn by watching videos that are part of the curriculum.

Auditory: let them listen to audio or video content like audiobooks. Let music be played as background (if they don't get distracted by it). Review books and ideas instead of asking the children to read. They should then note down their answers.

Tactile: Let them "try" rather than "watch". Offer examples, if possible, in order that the students are able to feel and manipulate the objects. Utilize manipulatives in math lessons.

Chapter 6: Evaluating lessons

If you're preparing or review lesson plans, make sure you keep these concepts to your mind. These are the factors that can increase your participation and learning:

Multi-sensory is simply the term used to indicate that multiple senses are involved when you learn the subject. As an example, listening to the story followed by making a diagram or model will provide you with information on movement during your lesson in addition to allowing students to test their understanding of the subject by looking over the completed diagram or model. A classic method of multi-sensory learning is used to teach beginning readers. It is a method of practicing the sounds of letters generally using a pen and paper while creating the sounds. After that, the letter tiles are put together to form words, and the child practice phoning the words they've constructed. A few ideas for learning through multisensory could include listening to an audio story and watching a short video about the same subject.

Active means that the participation and movement of a few people is permissible, or is even permitted. The activity doesn't necessarily have to involve playing on a trampoline or doing laps. Even the movement of letters on a whiteboard allows the possibility of interaction and movement. The most active way to learn is by practicing times tables when jumping on a trampoline, or going up and down stairs. It additionally, it involves drawing a sketch on a book they've heard, composing mathematics problems on a white chalk board, and completing an experiment in science that is hands-on.

Creative means that the students have choices for the outcome of their efforts. When you request students to create a drawing of a book you've read but they give them a specific idea of how the drawing should appear like, or ask that they color the trees in green and the blue sky, then you do not allow creativity to flourish and students won't be able to fully participate in the task. Let them have as much freedom as you are able, using just a few general guidelines for creativity so that they are able to incorporate their ideas in the work.

Meaningful meaning means you are learning in the course of activity. Meaningful activities can differ depending on the child. If your child is not a fan of drawing, the idea of drawing an illustration of a tale you've read might not be beneficial, but it might bring up the details of the story that you didn't know existed for other reasons. This also implies that asking questions that help them think about the main idea or event within a story could help, however giving the entire page of simple answers or demanding four different assignments on the same story may not be the best idea. It is important to ensure that your project is in line with the objective of understanding the subject and is not overly demanding as "busywork".

The word "changing" means you are using different ideas or techniques over the course of time. This might mean that you rotate of math-related activities, from worksheets through computer-based training to a board game. Or the fact that book summaries in October can be presented in the form of artwork or a brochure while in November presentations are put together. The degree of change as well as the type of activity used will depend depending on your student's interests and abilities. It is important to note that changing requires an alteration in the procedure and output. So the use of colored pens isn't going to make a difference, while switching from a card game into an actual board game could.

Fun: it's hard to define. You'll know that when you observe it. However, it could appear to be difficult to find on certain times. In general, I think that children love learning and exploring new ideas as well, and if you apply the ideas listed here, having enjoyment will naturally be an result, if not all often. You should also observe the activities your kids engage in during their free time to have enjoyment, and then try to integrate some of these things into your school curriculum (but not making them too specific or mandatory that they hinder their enjoyment during other times). If, for instance, your daughter is a fan of coloring and draw on her own time, you should try to include certain coloring or drawing activities in your school work too. My son is extremely active and likes to race around climbing trees, run around the yard, and leap across furnishings... therefore we incorporate trampolining, obstacle courses as well as laps (where the child has to sprint across the lawn or touch a tree ascend the slide, then jump off the slide's platform before running back to complete a maths problem to earn"points. "point").

The word "challenging" means the subject matter isn't fully grasped yet and needs an effort of the learner to accomplish. It's easy to get over the challenge by either giving the material too challenging or by providing too much. However, children love the accomplishment of solving problems the same as we do adults. So include challenges wherever possible to make them feel that they've made progress in the final day. If your child begins getting angry or frustrated it's probably too difficult. Reconsider the amount or the difficulty or even sit down alongside them and offer suggestions or guidance to assist them in solving the problem.

Chapter 7: Basic Principles

Before getting into the different subjects and techniques I'd like to talk about the fundamental principles that are applicable to every subject. Students who are clever or possess a great deal of energy tend to be at ease with having to sit for long periods of time working on subjects they are already familiar with and comprehend they tend to be dissatisfied when the volume of repetition, or "seat time" is high. In order to keep them happy and enthused, I've found some of the following tips beneficial:

1. Find out what the experts know prior to you get started

I always try to evaluate the present degree of my knowledge prior to diving into any subject, making sure that we're not retelling information which is well-known. I have been purchasing assessments in reading and math from Lets Go Learn to make sure we are making some progress each year, and to identify specific holes in knowledge that we need to fill in. I also use pre-tests when they are available prior to purchasing any new items for the curriculum.

2. First, get the wiggles out.

There is a tendency to perform some kind of activity prior to beginning in order to improve the focus of our minds and help us get any wobbles out. If you're looking for the more strict P.E. program, I found that the Family Time Fitness homeschool program is excellent. However, I must confess that we used the program occasionally. You can read more about it at was a lot more likely for me to request them to complete an obstacle course through the backyard, perform 100 trampoline jumps or to play Wii for 20 minutes whilst running around in a circle.

Additionally, I have a handful of my kids that are susceptible to refined carbs as well as sugar. They are prone to collapse if they do not consume a substantial and sugar-free breakfast. If you notice that your child is having problems at school during certain hours of the day, you might want take note of what your kids are eating and at what time. These kids are also likely to be irritable whenever they're hungry but they don't think that eating is at the root of the problem.

3. Make sure to keep it in smaller pieces

I'm sure if you've got little ones who get wiggly, you're already trying to divide tasks into small steps so that you don't overwhelm your students with. However, I've noticed that many of the programs are designed with more sections or assignments or include multi-page worksheets that can lead to a great deal of stress among my pupils. I look at our bigger school plan and split projects into smaller pieces, with management tasks to be completed each day. If we're involved in a bigger project, I try to find parts to work on that take only one or two days to finish, making them not as overwhelming.

If they have to do the same thing over and over again such as long division - it is one recent instance I'll print an entire page of questions, and ask them to choose one or two of them daily from the page. This allows me to ensure you get the necessary practice without making my kids feel overwhelmed.

4. Variate the method and methods

A lot of skills need practicing before becoming easy for smart and confident children often don't have the patience to practice. If you are able to make the process more varied it will be easier for them to learn before becoming bored or grumpy.

In particular, we faced the most difficult task of learning times tables in this class. I had hoped it'd be straightforward and so I initially bought several flash cards, and planned every day practice until they could be easily memorized. Naturally, it was not the case!

My kids are able to memorize their times tables but this wasn't because of the flash cards. We began modifying our methods frequently, which made a huge difference in our scores rapidly. The things we implemented:

* Prizes awarded for correctly completing the multiples of certain numbers.

* Reciting multiplications while jumping over the trampoline.

Competitions with flash cards, where the player who correctly answers retains the card, and the winner with the greatest number of cards wins.

* Times Attack (an online program at http://www.bigbrainz.com/)

* Multiplication Rap DVD

Different methods can be helpful for children who have difficulty with learning something using traditional methods "standard" method, i.e. via listening or reading a workbook. Through listening or a workbook, the more the elements of writing, music, projects using color code or humorous rhymes songs, the better they'll learn.

5. Make sure to do hands-on work whenever possible.

Certain kids can learn best using videos or books however, I have found that my children become bored or disengaged before they've completed the class. Our learning was more successful in math when we built challenges using manipulatives, or when we pulled plants out of the ground, and then sketched out the various parts on an affixed piece of paper. Another benefit of working with hands is the fact that students will typically work on their lessons even beyond the time that formal instruction is finished, if they have found engaging work.

6. Be calm and remember that they're making progress!

If you work with a book you will easily determine the place you're at... when you're halfway through the workbook, then it is likely that you're at the grade! The work of a project is more difficult to measure... Does the creation of Roman armor actually help you get towards the conclusion or the end of a chapter? Be aware that adulthood requires many talents which aren't all the ones can be documented in a manual. Knowing that carrying a sword throughout the day can be very exhausting is a great way to increase their understanding of the past as wars have been taken on the strength and endurance of soldiers! Also, taking apart the clock before put it back together can help them understand the fundamentals of how clocks work more than any other video could ever.

Believe in the process Keep them enthusiastic about the process, then attempt to take a breather, knowing the abilities they're acquiring will be helpful later on and the skills acquired through hands-on activities will last for a long time.

Getting Started

Set long term goals first.

Before you dive into the techniques or curriculum, spend the time to record your expectations for your child. If you can, use broad longer-term goals for starting and write down the areas you think they will be able to do as they leave high school.

Examples of long-term objectives could include:

* Ability to comprehend and read the complexity of details

* Ability to apply math in daily situations like at the grocery store

Ability to communicate effectively, which will be required in job scenarios.

• The capacity to be able to interact with others through both writing and verbal communication. writing

Ability to cook, tidy the home, mow a lawn, maintain a vehicle and repair basic things in the home

The issue may not align to the standard goals of the public school system in which goals are linked to particular skills for a specific grade or age the relevance of these skills for life post-high school isn't usually considered. If you thought that the public schools were the right fit for your child, I'm sure that they'd be there! If you're homeschooling think about the wider perspective of your life too.

Consider the things that need to be done this year.

After you've established your longer-term objectives in mind Consider what you need to be done in the coming school year that will help you achieve the targets. This is the time to choose your curriculum for learning or method, to ensure that your actions will help continue to progress towards your goals for the future. It is crucial to do this if your child is unruly and can only spend a small amount of time doing academic work - this way you will be able to make sure that you are using your time most efficiently in reaching your goals for the long term.

However, I am aware the possibility that there are specific state mandated standards or exams to pass - therefore, include them in the plan. Certain states have attendance requirements and monitoring of time spent in addition to time spent tracking - if that is the case for your particular state, be sure to keep your eyes on learning-related actions like walks through the neighborhood while reading the contents of a book or educational films can all be counted towards the required time therefore you don't require your student to be tied to a chair during all the hours of each day!

Then, choose a suitable program and activities.

After you've decided on your objectives for the year, have a take a look at the available curriculums and determine how you'll develop your curriculum during the course of the entire year. There is a possibility of purchasing an already-constructed curriculum and make a list of subjects to be covered or read, and figure out how you'll accomplish those goals.

Chapter 8: Making Subjects Active

When you've crafted your plans for your student It's now time to decide the curriculum you'll use or your methods of the entire year. This article will discuss a range of choices to consider, including selection of curriculum options and resources / suggestions that can be used to create or enhance classes.

Early Reading

Reading can be difficult for a lot of active children because there's quite a bit of understanding that they require before they are able to be able to comprehend anything that is interesting.

If you are looking for a complete learn-to-read multi-sensory program, we found 2 that we liked: "Primary Arts of Language" and "All About Reading"

They both have a wide range of activities to help children enjoy the process, as well as being scripted to ensure that they do not require too long to prepare for parents. They both need you to be alongside your child during all of the lesson. This could be time-consuming, particularly in the case of teaching multiple lessons.

A similar program that is easy to use can be found in "Reading Reflex: The Foolproof Phono-Graphix Method for Teaching Your Child To Read" written by Carmen And Geoffrey McGuinness. This book includes instructions written for the early letter sound pairs, and they have pages that you print and cut letter cards in order to help your child organize the letters that they have learned into simple phrases.

Some chubby kids have the ability to stay focused on computer-based games for an incredibly long duration. If you have one of these who is learning to read - look into the Reading Eggs online program (http://www.readingeggs.com).   My "wigglers" happily spend 20 to 30 minutes per every day working on the program, and they definitely noticed improvements regarding reading abilities.

Reading Improvement

After children learn how to read, their next step is to encourage youngsters to stay still enough to be able to read independently!

If you are able to get your child fascinated by popular titles search online for studying guidebooks. In particular, there are plenty of guides for well-known shows like Harry Potter as well as Percy Jackson. You can also get them to speak to you the principal ideas, characters descriptions as well as summaries and alternative conclusion ideas. Be cautious about the addition of many different activities to the "fun" book, as it could turn reading less enjoyable. At first the development of a love the habit of reading may be much more important than the particular books that are read.

If you truly want them to be able to read classics but they are more interested in Percy Jackson, consider listening to them on audiobooks before working on the related lessons to differentiate them from the personal reading. We've borrowed a variety of audiobooks from libraries that we played in the car when we were running errands such as "Charlie and the Chocolate Factory", "The Borrowers" as well as "Ralph and the Motorcycle".

Literature can also be introduced through Jim Weiss CDs (http://www.greathall.com). He has abridged versions the more challenging works, like Sherlock Holmes as well as Shakespeare and also CDs with stories based on these works that range in length from Greek Myths to the Arabian Nights to an account of Abraham Lincoln.

Evan Moor Daily Reading Comprehension is a good choice for kids. The books are simple, one-page worksheets, each with a fascinating or humorous passage, and a few concerns about the passage. The worksheets were short and engaging enough for us to finish them with no hassle longer. They are available in printed form through most homeschool supply sites and Amazon.com, or available for pdf download from Curr Click (http://www.currclick.com).

Reading Detective is a similar product designed for elementary school and older children, since they require to comprehend a passage of text for them to be able to use it. The program requires reading a text in order to answer comprehension questions, then specifying which paragraph provided evidence to support the answers. They can be a great way to prepare into college entrance tests afterward. These are sold by the Critical Thinking Company (http://www.criticalthinking.com/).

It is useful - it helps improve vocabulary and gives children the impression that reading is enjoyable as well as useful. It's also enjoyable! It is possible to do "double duty" on this issue by reading science or math-related readers. A few of the most popular math books are those from the "MathStart" series and Sir Cumference The two collections are readily available at libraries, or on Amazon.com. For Science Readers there are sets of books available from Scholastic on topics like animal habitats, human body systems and earth science (store.scholastic.com).

The main thing you need to do when reading is understanding the text, something that allows you to become very imaginative using. Here are some suggestions for you to consider:

• Read a story, and ask your students to create charts that show the beginning of the story - middle and ending

Create a scene in the tale and explain the scene to yourself

* Create a diorama

Create a drawing or model of the main character in the story.

We will tell you the tale in a concise format

You can watch a film with similar story and examine the similarities and differences between them (a Venn diagram is an effective method for students in the younger grades)

• Create a stage play which focuses on the major points of the plot

• Design costumes that are based on fictional characters and explain how events unfolded through their eyes

Writing

I'm not sure there is a NEED to spend money on a curriculum in order that teaches children to write however, I have personally I found it difficult to write without guidance from an instructional program.

If you are teaching them directly and directly, there are a variety of graphic organizers that are available on the internet to download for no cost. They also serve as fill-ins that are fun (think "MadLibs") to help students understand the different elements of speech and a self-editing checklists for students to be able to assess their writing. Children also enjoy creating their own stories. One of my sons wrote a number of books for his younger sister and then added graphic images taken from the web.

Druidawn (http://www.creative-writing-solutions.com/legends-of-druidawn.html) is a role playing based writing program, where students have to write each week to give their character new skills and to "battle" - sort of like a text based video game. It has been a great experience for me in working with an unmotivated writer using the program. There is a requirement for a monthly installment but it's also very much a hands-off program for parents. You could also create your own role-playing writing curriculum with others of the same age.

WriteShop (http://www.writeshop.com) is a writing curriculum with a significant hands-on component to it. It contains graph organizers, lessons with scripts as well as methods for "publish" the works when completed. The elementary levels range from A-E, which include K to about the 5th grade as well as two higher grades that correspond to high school and middle school.

If you feel you need formal grammar exercises for your older elementary to middle school student, Winston Grammar (http://winstongrammar.com/) is a "hands-on" program with exercises involving colorful cards to analyze grammar, rather than sentence diagramming.

Math

I've learned that the average Middle School student who is not proficient in math is able to master all fundamental concepts throughout elementary school with around 40 hours. I'm not suggesting students to skipping math until middle School! But, I do share this since I do not believe that you should be worried if you aren't spending 30 minutes each day working on math along with your childish homeschooler. If you are able to spend just 5 minutes a day in school this is fifteen hours or more per year. So, you should be okay at the end of the day, maybe by doing a bit of catch-up every now and then.

Here are a few suggestions for teaching mathematics:

Curriculum:

McRuffy Math (http://www.mcruffy.com) is a good program for wiggly elementary age students. It has a few verbal math daily problems (which is possible to do by jumping around in the kitchen or standing up on their head) followed by one page of questions which focus on 2 to 3 distinct concepts. The program uses manipulatives if needed, only with a limited amount of overlap throughout the week.

RightStart Math (http://rightstartmath.com/) is a manipulatives-based program, and especially good for those where math is more difficult. Concepts are taught through their abacus. They are then worked on using the abacus until it makes sense to the students. Classes also contain activities, with the majority of them using their own decks of cards. My son has found them to be surprisingly enjoyable - recently we had a fun game where two players drawing cards to calculate a percentage, and then declaring them in the simplest possible terms. He then was required to inform me what was more significant. The player with the larger fraction won all the cards. It didn't look like a lot of an enjoyable experience to me! My son, however, wanted to play the game over and over again, and he got considerably more practice with the game than when he'd completed an exercise (plus I'm sure he liked it, therefore likely learned more).

MathUSee (http://www.mathusee.com/) is another manipulatives-based program. I was a bit puzzled by the order during the early years of their existence They spend an entire year focusing on adding and one year on subtraction for instance. But I love the use of manipulatives for the higher levels of math. Therefore, we switched to the course at the Pre-Algebra level. The courses are offered through Algebra 2.

Games: Games are an ideal way to work on mathematical concepts, without becoming a burden. There are board games available with different strategies as well as a guidebook on card games which offers lots of options to practice playing with a deck cards. In my home, I've noticed that "center" type games often employed in public schools is boring for our kids They usually involve the matching of games to math equations, as well as other "match-up" type activities. My children prefer an active, competitive game. Here are a few of our favorite games:

* Payday

* Exact Change

* Sum Swamp

* Yahtzee

* Totally Tut

* Math War

If you are looking to implement games for teaching directly - Here are some books that you can recommend:

* Mega-Fun Math Card Game, grades 3 - 5 (grades 1 and 3 also on sale)

* Math Card Games created by Joan Cotter (this is from RightStart Math and can be available on eBay as well as Amazon)

Activities that involve hands math concepts are easier to grasp for students by allowing them to use the concepts in real-world situations. Below are some examples of activities with hands on that can be used with the students

Store: Every family member takes a few things from their rooms for them to "sell". They set the price for their own items in turn, and each is able to become an "shopper" and "buy" (temporarily) items with the children. Make use of actual cash (coins) or even play games with money as payment to practice changing and adding money as well as writing down the purchase on the "receipt" and add them to. For older kids, you could introduce the concept of sales tax, for greater math-related enjoyment.

M&M statistics: Get an entire bag of smaller containers of candy that contain M&Ms and Skittles. There is a good chance you will find type of crackers with a shape to make use of in case you suffer from foods or sugar. Unpack each of the small bags and count the candy in it according to colour. Next, you'll need to work on ideas like mean, median, and probabilities using the data. In the end, allow them to eat a bit!

Physical activities: including an activity that is physically based to help with math is an excellent idea. As an example, they could recite maths facts as they jump on the trampoline and solving math-related or verbal exercises when walking through the neighborhood.

Books: A few recommended books is the "Sir Cumference" math stories written by Cindy Neuschwander, as well as the "MathStart" series. They have the benefit of being readily available through the library. Another enjoyable math-related book to read can be found in "One Minute Mysteries: 65 Short Mysteries You Solve with Math!" written by Eric as well as Natalie Yoder. It is a good idea to read the story in front of the class, then ask each student to decide what the answer was, starting by the smallest.

Practice online: We've utilized a variety of online math applications to help us practice. We have found the ones we like enough to be able to employ over many children as well as long stretches of time were:

* Prodigy (https://prodigygame.com/): This site has a game based on video game principles, where students "battle" and must answer math questions to attack. The game is completely free but a membership fee provides additional resources that can be used in the game. I

like this particular site as it comes with an online teacher portal that could be used to keep track of what your students have worked on as well as to establish suitable grade levels based on the types of questions they're asking.

* Timez Attack (http://www.bigbrainz.com/index.php): This program is a fun way to speed up math facts, including addition, subtraction, multiplication and division. The program is free to see whether it's suitable for your children.

* DragonBox Algebra (www.dragonbox.com, or download their applications at Amazon, iTunes or GooglePlay) The game is designed to teach fundamental algebra concepts through a way that is fun with levels that range from five and above as well as 12+.

* Math Blaster (www.mathblaster.com): This site has several different free games to improve math skills, and also links to purchase their games for Android or iOS.

Science

Science is among the subjects that is easy to get "hands-on", though it is also important for keeping the time needed to prepare to a minimum.

Curriculum:

Gravitas Publications (http://www.gravitaspublications.com/) offers a series of books which have brief text readings with high level concepts and advanced vocabulary. The series is that is geared towards grades K-4 that is titled "Focus on Elementary Science" as well as a more advanced one (intended for students in grades 5 to 8) known as "Focus on Middle School Science". Each of the series contains a textbook with a teacher's manual and a laboratory guide with activities on Chemistry, Physics, Biology, Geology and Astronomy. Additionally, there are testing and software to build an study notebook accessible. There is only one test for each chapter, which means you'll need to make your own experiments from websites or books on experiments.

R.E.A.L. Science Odyssey (http://www.pandiapress.com/publications/real-science-odyssey/) is another popular program for hands-on learning. It's longer than the previous one that includes hands-on exercises for every concept that is being taught. The programs offered include Life, Earth & Space, Chemistry and Physics for elementary school children, as well as Biology for middle schoolers.

"Sciencewise" from the Critical Thinking Company (http://www.criticalthinking.com/) is an inquiry-based program. Three books are included in this series. It is suitable to students in the 4th-12th grades. They include experiments as well as discussion of important topics that are relevant to science. They also use items you likely possess in the home. They're organized around an 2 page summary of each one that includes information on the supplies, instruction instructions, an understanding of what might happen when the experiment is completed and a follow-up question you can inquire from your students.

Resources:

If you would like to create your self-designed program, you can find a variety of options available on the internet with just a lookup. We created a mostly self-designed Chemistry course using hands-on activities to demonstrate each idea. Also, we've grown plants and removed them at various time points to examine the development of roots, as well as have raised animals ranging such as sea monkeys, ladybugs, chicken eggs and even ladybugs to study metamorphosis and development. A couple of good online resources are Insect Lore for any sort of insect kits (http://www.insectlore.com) and My Pet Chicken for lots of information on hatching eggs (http://www.mypetchicken.com). Home Science Tools was an excellent source of hands on materials at a reasonable price as well (http://www.hometrainingtools.com/).

Activities:

There are plenty of experimentation options that you can do hands-on while studying physics and chemistry - take a look at the books available from the library in your area, or use the Internet to search.

Caterpillars can be raised Ladybugs, frogs chickens while studying Biology. A different biology source that is excellent is "The Body Book" by Donald Silver. This book provides instructions for creating a child-sized body skeleton using brads and cardstock in addition to building models of each vital organ in your body while you examine them before connecting them to the body skeleton. In the end, you will are left with a complete representation of your body that you can hang on the wall.

Books:

There are some excellent options based on literature available to scientists and also for the following:

* "One Minute Mysteries: 65 Short Mysteries You Solve with Science!" Written by Eric as well as Natalie Yoder has brief "mysteries". It is possible to read the story aloud, then ask each participant

to figure out the answer starting at the smallest.

* Scholastic reader sets (store.scholastic.com) - sets are available on a wide range of science topics, including earth science, weather, the human body, astronomy, and animal habitats.

* Stories that relate to this topic like "Hill of Fire" by Thomas Lewis (a story about the eruption of a volcano in a farmer's field that is based on an actual historical incident).

• Biographies of famous scientists like "Archimedes and the Door of Science" as well as "Galen and the Gateway to Medicine" Written composed by Jeanne Bendick.

Chapter 9: Social Studies

The social studies curriculum in the elementary and kindergarten grades usually comprise of units that focus on the way people interact and the various occupations that people could have. The class read a few stories on jobs like doctors or firefighters from the library. When it came to interactions, I typically made sure to mention things I saw on my the field and on errands in order to show them the process by which, for example that the harvest of a farmer could be served on the dinner plates.

It became my favorite subject when we moved to mostly oral classes. It is true that the use of dictation, copywork and the writing of longer-length papers are good teaching methods, but they did not work for my exceptionally energetic students.

Curriculum:

"Story of the World" is a collection produced by Susan Bauer. The series can be purchased at many different places, including Rainbow Resource Center or Amazon.com.

We watched the lesson via CD rather than studying the lessons. After that, we answered the discussion questions from the book by speaking. If map-related work was offered for my children, I handed them the map using markers or crayons, as well as read the directions for them to colour the map. Also, we did what they loved during each chapter. It comprised all cooking as well as armor making, but not all coloring and crafting projects.

There's a wide range of amazing projects in the Activity Book that you can choose from according to the interest of your children. Additionally, we included activities that are hands-on which included making a complete collection of Roman clothing and armor and making a catapult that works from popsicle sticks.

"R.E.A.L. History Odyssey" (http://www.pandiapress.com/publications/history-odyssey/) is another hands-on series. These are essentially studies and activities guides that are designed to be the use of literature which require the purchase of other titles to be read. They provide a chronological overview of history as well as writing and reading assignments, maps, and other activities.

Once we moved to U.S. history, we found the series "All American History" (widely available; 2 places to start would be the Rainbow Resource Center (http://www.rainbowresource.com/) or Amazon.com) to be interesting and hands-on. Unfortunately, it doesn't have an audiobook edition accessible. However, it does include an activity guide packed with exciting projects. We added materials taken from Kaleidoscope Kids. Kaleidoscope Kids series mentioned above and more.

Activities:

If you don't want purchasing curriculum, the subject of you can certainly cover history by reading books at the library as well as projects on the web. The best results have been achieved when reading out the text and then listening to the story on CD and working with maps as well as projects that relate to the topic of discussion.

A great option is an excellent option is the Kaleidoscope Kids from Williamson Publishing. It has titles like "Going West! : Journey on a Wagon Train to Settle a Frontier Town" and "Pyramids! : 50 Hands-On Activities to Experience Ancient Egypt". The list of these on Amazon.com (search for Kaleidoscope Kids) as well as a lot of them are at my library. They provide interesting details regarding the subject and lots of projects that can be done hands-on for you to get more information about particular subjects.

Other good books that you could make use of for an unit study strategy:

The Hands-on Activity Guides of Laurie Carlson (More Than Moccasins, Colonial Kids, Pioneer Days More)

* "You Wouldn't Want to Be A _" Series (various authors)

* "Spend the Day in Ancient Egypt / Rome / Greece" Series by Linda Honan

* "How Would You Survive As ... " Series by Fiona McDonald

* "A History with 21 Activities" Series (various authors)

* "If You'd Be there ...", "If you Were There In the Year ...", "If you Were There In The Time ..." The Series (various authors)

* Kaleidoscope Children's books(various authors) with a variety of topics such as China, Egypt, Lewis & Clark and Knights & Castles.

It is possible to add activities to help bring the period "to life" - with costumes, a performance of significant occasions, or cooking activities. These books that we mentioned that are for unit studies have lots of interesting suggestions as well as discover fun ideas on the web. We've had a few ideas before:

* Created a set comprising roman clothes (from an old bedsheet) and a the helmet (cardboard as well as duct tape) and a sword (PVC as well as cardboard, duct tape and). We acted like roman soldiers and prepared an ice-cream sandwich with

the oven (over the flame of a BBQ is more authentic!). Watched "Engineering An Empire" video on Rome.

* Made an Egyptian costume (from an old bedsheet) as well as the collar (cardboard with a marker, and put-on jewels). Made lentil rice pilaf. Learn about "Egyptian Diary: The Journal of Nakht" written by Richard Platt and "The 5,000-Year-Old Puzzle: Solving a Mystery of Ancient Egypt" by Claudia Logan (older kids) as well as "Tut's Mummy: Lost...and Found" by Judy Donnelly (younger kids).

When it comes to economics, my children have had a great time and learned lots of information in "How To Build Your Own Country" written by Valerie Wyatt. The book explains how you can create your own country (your room maybe?) including laws, a flag along with currency, as well as a means to generate revenue for your citizens. My oldest son has just declared his room to be a sovereign state, and created the country of his choice which includes legislation, currency and a national flag at the entrance. He worked all day doing the work learning a great deal and had a blast.

Art and Music

I wanted my children to get an education in music and art that was formal instruction, however, I do not have the knowledge to accomplish this by myself. As a rule, once they were sufficiently old and interested, we'd provide them with lessons which meant these were in-home exercises to help them gain an understanding of the subject.

There are a number of good DVDs which teach skills for artists through short, focused classes. Two options are Home Art Studio
(http://www.officialhomeartstudio.com/)

and Atelier (http://www.homeschoolart.com/).

Maestro Classics CDs (http://www.maestroclassics.com/) are classical music stories such as The Nutcracker, Peter and the Wolf, and Swan Lake. They integrate classical music into stories, and be enjoyed in the automobile.

"Those Amazing Musical Instruments!" by Genevieve Helsby is an interactive CD that focuses on the instruments of an orchestra. It also includes audio clips, interactive elements and functions.

Make your yourself musical instruments by using the guide book "Make Your Own Musical Instruments" written by Anna-Marie D'Cruz. I've seen a variety of designs to build instruments online such as the drums that are made of oatmeal canisters as well as shakers that have beans in them.

Foreign Language

The process of learning a new language isn't easy. It is possible to increase the enjoyment of studying it by interacting with people who speak the language, or through games at your home. In the case of, say, you've covered foods within your course, work out how to speak a couple of basic words - like "please pass the " - after which you can eat your dinner and attempt to communicate with the other person in that one. It will help you practice greetings, simple questions and responses, as well as a pleasant break from your daily routine.

There are also excellent DVDs to choose from Here are some that we recommend:

* Spanish for Kids: Series created by Sara Jerez and Jorge Anaya

* Spanish for Kids Series taken from Language Tree

* Rock N Learn: Spanish

* Little Pim Spanish

"Nature for Kids": Get Spanish through Language Tree

PetraLingua is a PetraLingua program is a comprehensive curriculum for children in the elementary grades as well as multi-sensory. It includes videos, books and activities. Learn more on it on their website, www.petralingua.com.

Mentoring

Mentoring is a great option to offer your students practical, hands-on knowledge as well. If they show a keen desire to learn about a particular topic take them on the opportunity to go on field trips or meet experts from the field they might be able to speak with. Sending an email to an expert containing specific questions have resulted in some great talks with experts within our own home.

This can be an excellent option to let them get practical skills that you cannot do by yourself. A grandmother who knits, an acquaintance's father who is a woodworker or an acquaintance from work with a print shop are all possible tutors to your child.

Chapter 10: Finding Your "Why"

When you are beginning to homeschool the first step is understand the reason you are choosing to do it. There are a myriad of great arguments and good ones.

The 5 most important reasons to use

• Create a positive social space away from bullying and pressure from peers

* Develop a more personalized method for your child's education

* Create an atmosphere where children are excited to learn

* Get a stronger spiritually-centered education

* Make room for greater flexibility in the family life

Whatever the reason the case, you must fully understand the "why." There can even be several factors, but it's important to know the purpose of them.

Understanding the "why" will help you choose the right way to teach your children at home. There are many methods and theories (which we'll explore in the next chapter) Sometimes, you'll find that your "why" will lead you towards a plan that can meet the requirements for your household.

The motivation behind homeschooling could serve as a motivation in times of stress. There are going to be difficult times on the homeschooling journey. From children who are sick to being unable to concentrate and feeling as if your home was struck by a storm and never cleaned again. There are days where you're just a little bit irritated If your children play with you for a second time and you snap, it could be a sign of frustration. It's the truth. There won't be a perfect day all the time

However, there are bound to have days when homeschooling can take a toll. Knowing an understanding of your "why" clear in your brain helps you deal with those days, and also motivates you to continue regardless of when you begin thinking about sending your children to a public school for the day.

What really helped us as we began the homeschooling process was the writing of the mission of our homeschool. This document outlines the way we'd like education and the way we live at home. It is a way to keep us focused, assists us in focusing on what we truly intend to teach our children and how exactly we would like to achieve it.

It is highly recommended that you think about making your mission statement. What would you like your dream home, family as well as learning experience to look like? Create it, then build it together as a family and incorporate it into your everyday life. It will make everybody within your family know the goals you're aiming for and reinforces the importance of your "why."

The fact that you have a mission statement does not guarantee that things will run smoothly. However, when everything is running smoothly, you are able to take a look, reorient your direction and help bring your family back on course. Take a moment to grab a pen and notebook, record the reason why you are there and begin making a mission declaration. The statement doesn't need to be long however, it must be focused and clear.

Who Can Homeschool?

It's possible that you're contemplating, "This is all fine and dandy, but am I really qualified to teach my kids?"

Yes! If you've got the high school diploma or the equivalent, you're better than qualified to guide your children in the comfort of the home. You have a better understanding of your children than anyone else. You are aware of what they love and dislike, when they're excited at school, bored, excited, nervous, or bored. Your children know what they like. If you don't want to stop them from becoming the very best version of them, you'll have a good time. Two teachers say that (and we're serious about it!

The truth is that teachers attend school to discover a variety of things regarding learning. A lot of this information about psychology is available through an internet lookup (types of intelligence as well as learning styles, modifications for those with disabilities or disabilities, etc.). However, that's only one course. A majority of classes revolve around ways to make a specific topic more engaging, interactive, or even more hands-on. Other lessons are focused on managing every student. Seriously. I took a whole yearlong course on creating habits that work and how to prepare your classroom for success, and also how to handle behaviours. These aspects are crucial in the case of thirty 6-year youngsters within your class. In schools where the teacher is the sole adult who is in charge of a vast class of students and must to persuade the kids that the subject matter he/she talks about is exciting and fun and they must pay attention and behave.

In a school that is public, it can be like being the only adult attending a kid's birthday party that has 30+ students and having to make them sit down and complete work in order to show they know the subject matter you're talking about. Most of the time it's like they're not even thinking about what you're going to talk about!

If you homeschool there are only your children. They are yours to know. You can tell if they had enough rest last night, whether they've had a decent meal and whether they were involved in an argument with their sibling that day. They know what they love and are fond of and their biggest pet peeves. Your kids are yours. Your homeschool can be customized so that your children fit just like a glove. Choose the textbooks they are most interested in. It is possible to study subjects which they're genuinely interested in. The learning can to fit into their daily schedule, having breaks for illness and not stressing about needing to do their homework. I am confident that every parent has the skills to help their child learn.

However, what happens if you aren't sure you're competent to instruct a particular topic? Perhaps you're not great in math or do not remember much about the War of 1812. That's okay. One of the best things you can do for your child is to tell them, "I don't know, but let's learn it together!" Sincerely There is nothing more exciting for children than knowing that you as the parent, aren't experts in everything, and being eager to discover new things! Therefore, you should read the book to your child. Let them search for things via Google or look up interesting video clips on YouTube. Most curriculums have "teacher" manuals that walk you through activities and lessons. If you're concerned regarding your abilities to teach the subject you are interested in, look for a course that comes with a manual for teachers.

There's also lots of support available. With the advent of internet technology and the internet, you can find classes, online schools as well as programs to join for. From complete curriculums to one-off "masterclasses," education has been digitally transformed in the last decade. There are a myriad of ways you can let someone else instruct or assist your child in a particular area or topic. If classes in person are you prefer, take a look at classes offered at the library, community centre, or even a community college welcome to dual credit courses for high school! Find a co-op in which parents share the responsibility of teaching what they're good in. It's not just about "academic subjects" either. There are leagues for basketball at home and karate classes, arts and science days, as well as cooking lessons. The saying goes that it is a community effort to bring up the child. That's especially true in the case of schooling at home. The fact that "home" is in the wording, does not mean your child will only be able to learn in your home.

Is This Even Legal?

Most of the inquiries we receive are related to the legality of homeschooling. There are several factors that contribute to the confusion around lawful homeschooling. The first is that homeschooling is a legal option throughout Canada as well as the United States. However, each territory, province as well as state will have their own laws.

The second reason is that a lot of teachers, principals, as well as social workers don't have the knowledge on the law governing homeschooling. It is possible to hear accounts of principals, teachers as well as social workers trying to convince parents away from teaching their children at the home. They claim they're worried about a child's requirements and socialization, or their security. It is believed that they are looking to defend their positions as they continue pushing children through the educational system.

It's possible that this is an issue, but as a teacher I consider this to be few and far in between. Teachers and principals generally aren't aware of the homeschool laws like you wouldn't have any knowledge of laws pertaining to property if you weren't particularly connected to this world. The majority of them are looking at what they believe is the best option for their child, and as they are aware of nothing about the homeschooling process, they are concerned. However, it's not their concern. Your decision is up to you and you are entitled to remove your child from the school system and teach yourself at the home. In light of the general inexperience with the rules of homeschooling, many parents find themselves overwhelmed and confused after leaving the educational system. Another cause for disorientation is the fact that there exist numerous situations to consider that each may require an entirely different method regardless of the region or city.

A great example is found within our own province, Ontario In Ontario, there are three scenarios that the majority of people face.

1. Your child has not attended school (never had a school record ....ever). There is no need to report anything to any person.

2. Your child previously attended a school located in Ontario but you've decided to drop from the program. If this is the case it is necessary to submit an official letter to

the school board informing them that you will be in the process of homeschooling your child. It is only legal to submit this form once for each child.

3. A few parents write a letter of their intentions to the school board every year due to the need for a formal acknowledgement letter from the school board due to various motives (to avail various therapy options or divorce cases, for instance, an alleged history of truancy, as well as Child Protective Services).

It is evident that in a region with lots of options for homeschooling, there's the possibility of confusion. Parents may end up writing every year a letter. However, this isn't required. You might be worried that even though you do not require the letter of acknowledgement right at the moment, you may need one later on. In reality, it's entirely your decision to be in the present situation so it's your responsibility to do the best thing for your family.

It is legal across Canada and in the United States, as well in many other nations around the globe. The rules and regulations vary between countries.

We are in Ontario in Canada, where there are virtually no regulations. If your child hasn't gone to school, then you don't have anything to worry about.

However, just across the street to Quebec there are rules that are different. Quebec is known as one of the most stringent for homeschoolers. It requires students to learn the same things as colleagues in the public schools however, and only using approved curriculum. Additionally, they must pass a test or submit a portfolio annually for review.

The comparison merely highlights how diverse the rules may be in different areas.

Also, the rules are susceptible to changes. We suggest looking over the local regulations and rules in the early stages and gaining a thorough understanding of them. It is possible to join the Home School Legal Defence Association (HSLDA to shorten it) could be an excellent organisation. Although they're an affiliated religious organization with the Home School Legal Defence Association, they charge a nominal fee they provide legal assistance for those who homeschool and can give you details about the regulations for your province or state. There are a few states and provincial associations offering similar solutions. For instance, the Ontario Federation of Teaching Parents is one of them.

Chapter 11: Letter of Intent

It is a formal letter that states the intention to educate your child at home. There are numerous variations available on the internet. Simply print one out and fill it out complete it with your signature and then send the letter to your school board. Also, it is a good idea to forward a copy of this letter back to principal at the school you're taking your child from, particularly for the first time. Certain provinces offer a form to complete instead of a formal letter. They are usually available on the education site of your province.

Important to know that a lot of places will need to submit your application before. In the case of example, August 31, is the deadline to submit your application for British Columbia. If you do not make this deadline then you may not be eligible for all the tax-free rebates to homeschool in the province.

Learning Plan

Certain schools will require an outline of your learning goals for the year. It usually includes the list of subjects to be absorbed throughout the course of the course of the year, a curriculum as well as textbooks you'll be using and the major tasks that must have to be completed.

Portfolio

Portfolios generally are a compilation of an individual's most successful assignments. There are some areas that may require regarding the type of or many tasks should be listed. Include essays, math test or workbooks, a science project as well as social studies pages. Be sure to follow the guidelines of the local government or school board, and you'll be able to determine what's needed.

Testing/Assessment

Certain areas require that students be tested annually to make sure they're in the right direction and achieving appropriate levels. These are also dictated by each area. The board of your school or department will have information regarding the testing process and the date the test will be held. The department should also provide you with the list of subjects that could be addressed during the exam.

Reporting

The practice of reporting is also common. A lot of areas use reports or forms to be filled out on a regularly intervals and sent for the board of education. These are like an annual learning plan, however they provide more details on what you've learnt in the past few weeks. The school's board.

Deschooling

This is a section for parents who had a child in the private or public schools and who decides to pull the child away to teach themselves at the home. Deschooling refers to the process in the removal of your child from the educational system and provide them (and you) some time for them to settle into their new routine prior to hopping onto the school-to-home wagon. When you deschool the amount of (if there is any) education that takes place. It's the time to get rid of the notions about your notions of what a school day is and instead focus on the kind of learning that will be like in the coming years.

There are many aspects to deschooling, and they are all based on the reason your child's no longer attending school. If your child quit the public school system in the month of June, and hasn't decided to go back for religiously based education Your deschooling program could take two months in the course of the summer. However, if you're doing your homeschooling because your children struggle and don't like going to school, the deschooling duration may be longer in order to give the child to develop their perspective and understanding of how to teach.

In most cases, 2-3 months suffice for time, however some can go as long as 6 months. There are some who recommend 1 month per year for each year of school (so the second-grader gets 2 months and a 9th-grade student would receive nine months). You are the parent to determine how you want to extend this duration. It's equally crucial to set some timeframe, or else it's possible to let the process of deschooling continue for a long time.

In this period the government should not issue any specific instructions. None. There is no formal education whatsoever. A lot of parents make use of the time of deschooling to concentrate on chores, family as well as life-long learning. Parents take their children on their trips to get groceries and appointments, wash the laundry, take hikes and cook, wash and read what they like and enjoy games.

A key part of deschooling allows you, as a parent time to figure out how you're going to submit all required documentation and find the program you'd like to follow and recognize that homeschooling doesn't mean the same as schooling at home. This is very different than school. Usually, it requires significantly shorter time (usually less than a few hours) as well as a lot of time for enjoy, play and explore the things they're passionate about and enjoy family life.

Also, it's a chance for kids to enjoy an opportunity to be free. After a long time within the classroom where every minute is planned out for them and they are in charge, staying home for the entire day could become difficult to handle. Deschooling helps them adjust to their new surroundings. Perhaps they'd like to see more television or play video games? Fine. Allow them to enjoy all that liberty out of their lives. In time, they'll begin looking for new activities to take part in that they're attracted to.

Children sometimes succumb to the demands of schools and their peers to enjoy something that they do not like. The deschooling process offers them the chance to truly be themselves. They will discover what they are really like and what interests them. Do they really enjoy Pokemon or are they simply interested because the other students at school were. Perhaps they'll realize that they truly love the space world and all its adventures!

It is also possible to discover their normal routine. There are many kids who suffer from insomnia getting up early in order for the bus ride to school, and going to bed late following the completion of extra-curricular activities as well as homework. In this time of deschooling it is possible that your children are sleeping longer and sleep later. In reverse. You'll discover your own natural rhythm, and then adjust it with time. You can then create a homeschooling schedule that fits you and your kid's schedule and habits instead of forcing them to conform to an appropriate time. Perhaps you have a child who does not like mornings, so having school in the afternoon is preferable.

Chapter 12: Socialization

One of the concerns most homeschoolers are faced with is "What about socialization?" The answer we always give is, "What about socialization?" We've been asked that question by relatives, friends as well as my dentist and other random people in Chapters. It's one of the main concerns many people have concerning the homeschooling process. However, in reality, it's really not a problem at all.

The history of homeschooling is long. Before 1900, lots of kids were educated in their homes. Then, mandatory education became an option to keep children away from dangerous factories and, as a result was the standard.

The notion that socialization occurs exclusively in classrooms is a new idea. It was actually in the latter part that of the twentieth century. Our belief is that the issue stems in the name. Children who go to public schools generally reside located in two locations in their homes, or in school. If people hear "homeschool" they often think, "well the kids are in their homes for the time of home, then at home during school time, so they are at house all day long. What can they do to be socialized when they're always in their homes?" Obviously, this notion that kids who attend homeschool are living in their home 24/7 all day long is one of the reasons for being concerned. Many people are shocked to learn that homeschoolers are often forced to quit their home. The majority of us are out of the house and meeting with friends 3 to five times per week. It is a common occurrence for homeschoolers.

Additionally, the idea that education is the only means to make a child feel comfortable is a fundamental error.

Socialization is the way in the person is taught how to be a member of societythe norms that are generally accepted as well as what's not. They learn to sit in the line to cash out instead of rushing at the counter. This is learning to be a good actor at a theatre (movie or drama) or music). Learning to conduct conversations who are respectful, polite and fun for everyone.

Being in a class with others of similar age isn't the same as socializing. It's not going teach kids how society operates and to become actively involved participants.

Perhaps, children in homeschooling have a better social adjustment due to the chance to be around people with different ages and with different people more frequently.

Naming your Homeschool

The process of deciding on names can be thrilling and fun If you do not have a clue where to begin it's fine! Certain families prefer to pick names that are based on the last name of their child or which tells a story of them. Some draw ideas from nature or the interests they have. Whichever you decide to choose it can be an excellent place to begin and get your ideas flow.

Apart from the fact that you can name your homeschool since it's entertaining to name your homeschool but some individuals must choose to do so and must name their homeschool in their local area. Make sure you find out what rules apply for your particular area.

The Homeschool Name Generator that can help you brainstorm some concepts for names. You can find it on our website at www.raisingatoz.com/homeschool-name-generator/.

Approaches

One of the most important things you'll find is the fact that there are many ways to go about it. They all claim to be the most effective method of teaching children at home.

Before diving into different ways of homeschooling, I'd like to get a couple of things very easy to understand. One thing is for certain, there's no way that will be superior to the other. There are countless blogs, podcasts, and Facebook support groups which claim that homeschooling is the best option and Charlotte Mason's method is the most efficient one, or that traditional education is the best way to create a strong basis to learn. This isn't the case. The individual's personality, values and convictions may lead you to one particular way of doing things however it doesn't mean that a different approach is superior.

The second reason is that very seldom does families fall under one homeschooling type. As we began our homeschooling adventure, I took an exam. It was one of those quizzes online that you take where you have to answer questions of multiple choice and then it gives you the homeschool approach the best fit for your needs. I tried it for enjoyment and was shocked to see that it said "Your style is Charlotte Mason." According to what I'd read at the time, it is not the kind of kind of style that appealed to me. However, as I sat down to read further and found the actual score of 25 25% Charlotte Mason, 24% unit Studies along with 24% unschooling and the remaining was split among various others types. The combination of styles fits my personality perfectly. We're adamant about a gentle educational system and believe that there are some important things to be aware of about life, however we are awestruck by following the passions of our children and let them pick their own subjects of their own. Also, we love the occasional fun unit occasionally also!

Don't be stuck with a certain type of style. A style may work for a couple of months or even a whole year, but it won't work with your family. That's okay. It's fine to change your personal style when your family grows.

With that in mind that, why choose an all-homeschool-style at all?

There are a few advantages to selecting a type. When you study an approach, you'll discover some excellent methodology and teaching techniques that are compatible in conjunction with the particular design. There are many styles that have specific topics, tasks or areas of focus. This can be useful if you don't have any clue about how to instruct. There are many book, support groups, and podcasts that are specifically designed for certain methods.

There are nine primary types of homeschooling, and every one is distinctive. However, there's a catch. The majority of people do not fall under the same homeschooling approach. As an example, you could be an Charlotte Mason homeschooler who loves the occasional unit study once in a while. The homeschooling community has one style that is predominant and often borrow a few things from other methods in order to develop the style distinctive as individual as their families. Here's a small amount of info about all nine different styles.

Classical

The oldest form of homeschooling, the classical method is a descendent of the Greek style of learning. The emphasis is on the study of facts and laws such as math, language, and logic. The emphasis is of learning the history in chronological order in order to be viewed as they change as they change and influence the world. It's a less rigid form of learning that places a focus on the study of Latin or Greek for the purpose of aiding writing and reading. Classical homeschooling is an old tried and tested method, and there are numerous curriculums available for use but it does require greater amount of sitting than different styles.

School at Home

That's precisely the way it is described. It's when you try to recreate the classroom environment at your in your own home. You'll find a schedule for the day of classes and times to each one. The school has recess breaks as well as lunch breaks. It is a common way that homeschoolers use in order to begin.

Chapter 13: Charlotte Mason

The name is a reference to the 19th century school teacher, this is an extremely popular choice, particularly for children in elementary school. It is based on the natural world, journalling as well as "living books" (books with stories, morals, and history that are all integrated) This is a more organized style than non-schooling, however less so as the traditional approach (while remaining a firm base of a child-centered curriculum). The style is also characterized by shorter learning time blocks (15-20 minutes for young children and 45 minutes for those in high school) and is which are followed by breaks, and then exploring the outdoors. It's a good way to integrate classical study or unit-based studies. This makes it the preferred choice of the majority of young homeschoolers. This style was originally designed to be a Christian homeschooling approach and many resources are religiously-affiliated. It can however be altered to be secular, if you choose to.

Unit Studies

It's a unique way of homeschooling. A theme, topic or book is selected for a set period of time, and all subject matter is viewed from that filter. So, for instance: Perhaps the theme of your period is sharks. In the month you'll learn about sharks, look at their teeth, and discover more about various shark species as well as their habitats, ocean living as well as conservation. Next month, you'll learn about the ancient Egypt in which you'll be taught about their culture, history as well as art and the best way build a pyramid on your personal. Learn about different rulers and queens. It's a format which is totally customizable for your child's preferences that makes it extremely entertaining.

Waldorf

The Waldorf educational system was created by Austrian philosopher Rudolf Steiner in the early 20th century. The school focuses on imagination, the arts as well as creativity and fantasies as well as a belief in the integration of the subjects of all disciplines through nature and art. They strongly believe in the early stages of storytelling, oral communication as well as imagination. Reading is usually delayed until the age of 2. The style is also focused on the natural resources like wooden toys, beeswax crayons and other materials that are natural, staying clear of technology and TV.

Montessori

The concept was developed by Italian doctor and educator Maria Montesorri in the early 20th century. The emphasis is on manipulatives and free-time This style focuses on teacher-led instruction as well as a more child-centric approach. A favorite among elementary school students as well as children with disabilities, as well as gifted kids, this approach is a great way to accommodate every kid on their own stage. This is a very physically and tactile method that is inspired by the environment. It also emphasizes artistic expression and.

Montessori isn't often considered the best method for homeschooling since it is a requirement to instruct Montessori it is necessary to be registered as a teacher within the company and go through the education. But, there's an increase in the number of homeschool parents who are applying the Montessori concepts into their homeschooling practices.

Unschooling

This style uses a child-centric approach. Children have full control over which subjects they'll study and the way they master the material. Parents act as mentors by helping their children learn. They can use the curriculum or worksheets but only when they are able to convince the child to participate in it, and it's based on their interests with an eye on. The art of sewing is an essential element of the unschooling process. It's a method of introduction to various topics as well as ideas, and then observing their interest in. Parents often provide opportunities to introduce children to new topics, yet leave enough facts so that kids can discover and expand their knowledge.

Radical Unschooling

The process of radical unschooling is very like non-schooling. It is the main difference that they do not follow any kind of curriculum. They don't have homework or workbooks whatsoever. It's that simple. Like children who don't go to school, they are devoted to the process of learning by living out all over the world.

Eclectic

It is also known also as Relaxed Homeschooling. This homeschooling design is unique to the people who use it. It's actually a mixture of different styles that are combined. Maybe you've heard that I stated that a lot of people employ several distinct styles? However, if they are predominantly into a single type, it isn't an eclectic approach to homeschooling. Homeschoolers who are eclectic use a mixture of various kinds of. They could conduct a unit study at times, and they may also disengage from certain subjects, but still apply the classical method to different topics. They explore different styles with ease in a way and "steal" things from various types to form an approach to homeschooling that is distinct and suited to the family they live with.

These are brief descriptions of the various styles and are not intended to be an exhaustive guide for each. It's just a starting point. If you find a particular aesthetic or a philosophy which appeals to you it's time to look at it further. Perhaps you're looking for a style that won't suit your family in any way. Move on and get rid of it.

The group we are Eclectic homeschoolers. We're a mix of Charlotte Mason, Unit Studies and unschooling, with a lot of arts and natural. We have found that it works well for us. There are several units as well as we have a Charlotte Mason math workbook and the majority of our social and science research. We have found this to be effective for us. However, there are others who are primarily traditional homeschoolers who adhere to the principles that is Charlotte Mason to a T. It's fine because this approach works for them.

I advise parents never to let their style box the way they dress and to accept adjustments if in the future, it doesn't fit with the goals of their families. However, every family must start with a place. Find a design which is suitable with your family's needs can be an excellent way to locate help groups, curriculum suggestions, resources, co-ops as well as inspiration.

Chapter 14: What To Teach

If you've made the decision to go homeschool You may be thinking, "What am I actually going to teach my kids?" In the case of where you live, this may be decided by the students. There are many states that have compulsory subject areas that you have to teach, with mathematics and language arts are among the most important on the list. There are many other subjects that you could teach.

Traditional Subjects

A majority of people are thinking only about the classic subjects. There's nothing wrong in this. There are plenty of subjects that you can educate children, and having the right education, which is well-rounded and balanced is essential.

* Literacy and Language Arts

* Math

* Science

* The Arts

* Social Studies

* History

* Geography

* Health and Physical Education

* A Second Language

Also, remember that every subject has to be taught constantly and for all age groups.

As an example, in Ontario schools Social studies are typically taught from Grade 6 onwards, and then it's time to switch to geography and history. They usually switch between these two classes. What's the reason I am saying this? because I want you to be aware that you do not have to be teaching all of these subjects every day. There will come a time that one falls naturally into your hands. Maybe it's the best opportunity to research cultural events (social research). Perhaps you have a child who has been captivated by Egyptian films. This is a perfect opportunity to learn about the story of early Egypt (history).

Additionally, there are some who like to dissect the subject even more. Language arts is a typical area with many sub-categories. Writing, reading, phonics and grammar. Spelling as well as cursive writing Latin. However, it is completely dependent on you!

Less Traditional (But Equally Awesome) Subjects

There are a myriad of fascinating subjects and topics that you could incorporate into your homeschooling. Incorporating various subjects is an awesome option to tailor your homeschooling to meet the needs of the interests of your kids as well as the values of your family.

Here's a checklist of items you may consider including in the homeschool curriculum of your children:

* Biblical/religious instructions

* nature studies

* Yoga

* baking/cooking

* life skills

* Coding

* Robotics

* the process of learning as a tool

* A specific sports (football soccer, football,, gymnastics, dance, etc.)

* crafts like sewing and quilting, and so on.

* jewellery making

* business/entrepreneurship

Blending Subjects

In reality, anything that interests children can become an area for them to learn about. This is the perfect opportunity to discuss mixing topics. The concept of project-based learning is very well-known. Like a unit, children are given the option of choosing an area of interest and then permit them to investigate as well as study all they are able to about the subject. You let them read books, go through videos and build models on the subjects they're fascinated by. Making a complete project around the subject is an excellent opportunity to get into the world of learning that typically covers a variety of areas (reading writing, reading or science, mathematics, history, etc.). It may sound like a lot of work, but it's really not as difficult as you think. If you build the baking soda-based volcano, there are many layers. The science isthe chemical reaction of vinegar with baking soda. It's also art when it comes to the sculpting and the painting of the volcano. Also, geography when talking about plate tectonics or the formation of volcanoes. It's a singular subject but encompasses a range of subjects and issues simultaneously.

Combining subjects can be a method to make learning experiences that span several subjects at the same time. Most activities and events involve multiple subjects but it's our job as parents to appreciate how subjects function in tandem.

As an example, we participated in an activity wherein we constructed tiny catapults and then released eggs. Eggshells were filled with paint, and then created abstract artwork. We merged art and science.

Also, we did an image scavenger hunt in our neighborhood looking for different companies. It was a combination of physical activity and photography (art) and the social sciences (learning about our neighborhood as well as businesses) as well as reading (looking at a list of businesses roads, signs for the road, and business signage). The activity was able to cover four subjects simultaneously and was extremely stimulating. Even our daughter speaks about it even during the coldest part of winter.

Chapter 15: Choosing Curriculum

One of the greatest challenges faced by homeschoolers is choosing the best curriculum for their children.

The first question is, do you really need to utilize a the curriculum? By curriculum, we're talking about workbooks and other educational programs available to help you homeschool. There's such a thing as having too many curriculum. There are too many books, which means that they spend long time at workstations. There are a few, including students who have little workbooks throughout the course of their children's education. They may also be radical, unschoolers who have no curriculum even. However, most homeschoolers at least use a few programs.

Do you also feel stuck in your education? The curriculum is an instrument. It's a tool you can use to assist your child while they acquire new skills as well as an opportunity to test these new skills. There are some curriculums that have timetables. You don't need to stick to them. It's not like you're a slave to books. They are yours to use however you want. Perhaps you'd like to begin at the beginning or end the chapter, then return. Your choice is up to your child.

How Exactly Do You Choose Curriculum?

This is a personal choice. Are you going to use workbooks, or an online course? Are you planning to use boxes sets or mix and match various choices?

In the beginning, you'll need choose what subject you'll need to create a course to cover. There are times when you'll need more help in certain areas. Many books include a wealth of information, advice and tricks. Some have practice books which contain only the bare minimum of information. The books you choose to purchase are your choice. There are also options for adding additional components. Certain curriculums are just the book, while some include a lot of additional features. Math courses are a good illustration. They are not all workbooks and others include a lot of manipulatives. Remember, more additional features you can add to the program you add, the more your program costs.

Do not be deceived by all of the extras. The additions aren't going to improve the quality of your program. If you're not going to utilize them, they're probably not helping. It's not a good idea to have a program that has a lot of manipulatives as we love using items that are lying in the home: Lego, seeds and toys, and cards. There is no need for additional features. However, if you'll be using these and believe they'll benefit you, then buying these products could be an excellent decision for you.

In the next step, you must select between religious and secular education. It's quite a challenge. For many decades, the top reason for homeschooling was religious instruction -- pretty much since the whole homeschooling-in-modern-day movement first began. This is why a lot of the most well-established programs are Christian-based. Today there are more Christian educational institutions than non-Christian. This means that you must determine if this is an issue for you.

However, not every Christian education is as demanding as some. If you're in search of an unrelated curriculum, be aware that there may not be as many choices.

It's not possible to give the complete listing of options for homeschooling since, frankly there are a lot of. From major-name brands to smaller business run by moms selling printed materials There are a myriad of choices. This is my top recommendation.

Talk to a friend. If you have friends who are homeschoolers, inquire about what they're using, and the reasons why they like the program. If you can, browse through their notebooks. Only ask those who you are familiar with. If you ask Facebook, it could lead you into a maze of possibilities that you were not looking for initially.

The more expensive option doesn't necessarily mean more effective - buying the most expensive course doesn't necessarily mean it will be superior.

Online reviews. I've stated that you do not ask Facebook for reviews, and I'm standing by that. However, do not avoid looking at the videos on YouTube. YouTube personalities, such as Rebecca from HomeschoolOn provide excellent reviews of a variety of different curriculums. She walks you through the textbooks, describing what's included in every package, and also who may or might dislike each one of the workbooks. Video tutorials are fantastic because they can see the inside of book and not be able to listen to 30 different opinions from people. I often check Rebecca's as well as other review of curriculum videos before purchasing any new books.

Create a budget. I strongly suggest you establish your budget prior to shopping for education. In the event that you don't, your costs will be a real shock. Choose the topics you wish to instruct and work to the next one.

Give yourself some room to move around There will eventually a point at which your course isn't working for you. Perhaps it's just too simple or too complicated or dull. Whatever the reason, it's no longer functioning. You shouldn't be a slave to it. When you allow yourself a bit of flexibility within your spending plan, you'll be able to have an opportunity to spend money on another item mid-year, when things aren't going as you planned.

If It Ain't Broke, Don't Fix It

There's a moment that every homeschooler experiences where they feel that they need to "change things up." The homeschool experience has become a bit monotonous and parents want to change the curriculum. In the event of dullness and the initial reaction of most parents is to change the course.

It's not an easy place. If you find that the curriculum is not really the right choice for your child (too simple, difficult or too much writing or just not engaging enough)

If so, it's best to shift curriculums. If your child is making progress, don't consider your curriculum the first item you alter.

It's easy to switch when you look at the most recent edition of this book, or the workbook your peers have been doing, or the gorgeously vibrant practice book which can make your existing plain black and white books seem so basic. Beware of being influenced. If the things you are doing is working do not alter the way they work.

If you find homeschooling to be a bit boring, you can try your curriculum. Consider a project that interests you and learn an interest or new skill with your family (watercolours and running, or even car mechanics) or add in some outdoors time, or add something to do during the week (hello poet tea time!). Make other adjustments to your daily routine. You might be staying home too often or out often. You can try tweaking the other areas prior to when you get into a mess with the curriculum, especially when it's working well for you. Parents aren't the only ones that change their curriculum after the dull time of their lives, and then buy a an entirely new program only to dislike it only to go back to their older choice afterward.

Scheduling and Planning

A lot of new parents who are homeschooling get overwhelmed with the task of arranging and planning the school year of their children.

It's important to emphasize that there's no "one way" or a "wrong way" to schedule. Each family is different and the way that works for us family may not be the best for you. Be prepared to alter your plans when things aren't working, or your family's situation is changing.

Chapter 16: Year-Round Versus School-Term Homeschooling

The term "school-term" typically refers to parents who educate their children for a certain period of time. This is like the public school system within the area they live in. In other words, you could decide to do your homeschooling between September and June (which corresponds to an identical model to the Canadian public school program). When you reach the last term then, you could enjoy a long breakwhich is a vacation in summer.

The term "year-round" schooling is just as it seems. Homeschooling is a continuous process. However, that doesn't mean you can't take breaks. Homeschoolers who are year-round take many small breaks during the course of the course of the year.

It's called the "Sabbath Schedule," where the school year is divided into six weeks of instruction and then have rest for a week (like God worked to create the universe for six days, and then rested on the seventh). This is great in some homes for the reasons of religion, others who are secular could also benefit from taking smaller breaks throughout the course of the entire year.

Which is Best?

There's no one right solution. It's all about finding what is best for you and your family. Selecting the right timetable for your homeschool is a personal choice. There are two options that work but only you are able to choose which one is most suitable for you and your family. Both have pros and cons for each one.

School-Term Homeschooling

Pros

* It is a public system. This allows you to take advantage of many programs such as camps for your kids

* You get an extra break to celebrate holiday

The longer break will mean that you will have time to organize, plan and place orders for items (supplies or curriculums) for the upcoming school year.

* A shorter school term implies that you will have a organized day with a rigid routine (in order to get everything into)

Cons

* The learning process can become lost during the course of summer.

* Reminds us that learning takes place at a certain moment, in a particular place and an exact manner

Year-Round Homeschooling

Pros

It is important to keep learning sharp as students don't experience long breaks that cause them to not remember what they've learned.

It promotes the concept that learning takes place "anytime, anywhere"

* Inspires love of learning and encourages the development of the capacity to be lifelong learners

* Lets children go faster

* Flexible and more relaxed program (3-day week, 4 day week)

• Easier to break away from markings and grades

Cons

* A less planned routine

* Can feel like school never ends

* You'll have much less time to prepare the next year

* Could be more costly such as when your child completes their schooling earlier than expected

Academic Terms

We recommend that all the homeschoolers include academics during their school calendar. This is a fancy method of saying that you need to divide your time into smaller chunks. This way allows you to have several moments throughout the year at which you are able to think about how your life are progressing.

There are three main types of breakdowns for school years: quarters, semesters, and term.

Semester: The half of a academic year (typically between 15 and 18 weeks) in which case it is possible to change the topics being covered. It is a common schedule in the high school.

Term: It is typically used in elementary schools, where classes are offered throughout the entire school year. The school year can be split into 3 periods. The duration of the term will be decided by the homeschooling or school parent. It is, in most cases an extended break (for example, a vacation following the third term).

Quarters: Three three month periods of time. This kind of timeline is frequently utilized by companies and financial institutions. However, a lot of homeowners who homeschool year-round like this plan for breaking down their school year.

The final day of the period or quarter can be the ideal moment to plan a series of activities to you succeed in your homeschooling. Choose your time, whether it's an afternoon, morning, or even an entire weekday (or even a whole week if you have to) take the time to do these four things to ensure that your homeschool is progressing.

Reflect

When you're done with your term, you'll be able to review the lessons learned and determine the things that worked and those that wasn't. It is possible to think about fixing the issues and adjusting your schedule so that it can more closely match your requirements or removing the curriculum altogether in favor of something completely new.

Regard the Future

Also, it's the perfect moment to think about the future and to make your plans more sturdy. Planning an excursion? It's the right best time to make it happen. Which books do you require during the coming months? Write a list and share it of your library's books so that they can be reserved.

Reset

The perfect opportunity to put your homeschool in order. We take the space at the conclusion of each school year to clean the homeschool space. We need to determine the supplies that are in short supply and replenish.

Record

A few states or provinces will require you to keep a record of the things your children are studying. Now is the time to update your record keeping, complete the files, and make sure you get your paperwork on track. It's a blessing to not have this type of obligation in Ontario However, I do keep a record of what has was working for us, and the things that did not. This way, when next year comes around I'm more equipped. I make a checklist of themes, ideas and trips. to be able to plan for the in the future. It is easy for me to reflect and look back at what my children loved and what did not perform well at all. As an example, we've realized that January isn't a great month for us due to the severe cold and the post-holiday downturn. After this realization it has taught me that I should create a fun unit study or topic for the month in order to keep us motivated throughout this period.

Another reason why you should make use of a break-down is to give yourself a deadline in case you're exploring something completely new. In the first few weeks, an entirely new course, program or program could be a bit bumpy. discomforts. That's okay. However, you shouldn't give up within a month. When you utilize a term or quarter, you are giving you a opportunity to determine if this is an issue of growth or the program isn't working.

In between year-round or school-term homeschooling, and the three various breakdowns, you have several ways to tailor your school year so that it is a perfect fit for your family.

Personally, we're all-year round homeschoolers who split our school year into three months (September until December, January-April and May through August). It works well for us. However, we have come across many homeschoolers that have various breakdowns for the year. Here are some of them.

* A homeschooler throughout the year who utilizes quarters, but begins their school year in the month of June. the school year ends, which means they're

doing more work in the academic area when museums, parks and science centres are full.

* A family with school terms that makes use of terms, and commences their school year in the month of August. It is finished before May, to allow for their strawberry farm u-pick business

High school students could take online courses which follow a calendar of semesters with some classes being offered throughout the year as well as other classes in the second quarter of the year. It's like many schools in the public sector. calendars.

Weekly Schedule

A lot of homeschoolers consider their weekly calendar to be one of their most crucial plans. This is a summary of play dates, field trips, doctor's appointments, and their learning time.

A few homeschoolers stick to the standard 5 day school week. They will do certain learning or work throughout the week, from Monday to Friday. A different model that is popular is the four-day school week. It gives you the opportunity in your work week that you can plan doctor's appointments and do errands, without feeling that you're "taking away from the kids' learning time."

Chapter 17: Blocks, Loops, and Everything in Between

A daily routine is likely to be a great idea regardless of what kind you decide to go with.

A block schedule is a way of having block of time set to each subject or activity. Here's an example

Breakfast 8:00 am

Math 9:00 am

Reading9:45 am

Writing 10:00 am

Science 10:45 am

Social studies 11:30 am

Lunch 12:00 pm

Outdoor Play 1:00 pm

Art 2:00 pm

Time of free time: 3:00 - 5:00 pm

Dinner 5:30 pm

Loops function a bit differently. The concept is to set up a sequence of subjects or activities that your child is able to engage in. After they finish one thing, you can move into the next. Once the loop is completed it's time to start again. The reason that people enjoy loops is that they allow the flexibility of. If your child requires extra time to study math, they may take advantage of that.

In order to demonstrate this the concept, we'll build a five-subject loop. Language, Math, Science, Art, Social Studies.

Monday, your child is doing Language, Math, and Science But the Math portion took a while.

longer. In the afternoon, you can run around and catch up with your friends

Tuesday. Your child should begin at the beginning of the second subject for the day, which in our case is Art

Today, they studied Art and Social Studies, and after that, they started the process again, and continuing with Language after which Math.

Wednesday They did Science, Art, and Social Studies

Thursday It was an extremely productive day, as the students studied Math and Language,

Science, and Art

Friday, your child was completely involved in your Social Studies lesson

Parents love loops since they are able to complete all of their classes within a week, and they won't be prone to forgetting the subject they're studying. Additionally, you are able to modify your loops to incorporate whatever you like. You can include handwriting, music practice, bible lessons, etc. The possibilities are truly endless.

It is also possible to have fixed subjects as well as a loop. As an example, if every day your child will have math and language homework to finish. After this, you can loop in different subjects or tasks. This is how it works.

Fixed - Language Arts and Math

Looped - Science, Art, Handwriting, Piano, and History

Monday Language and Math + Science and Art

Tuesday Language and Math + Handwriting, Piano, History,

WednesdayLanguage and Math + Science

ThursdayLanguage and Math + Art and Handwriting

FridayLanguage and Math + Piano and History

If you're more of an unschooler, or would prefer the absence of structure, then that's great as well! There are lots of families that have a flexible timetable or just have a handful of items that are scheduled for the time of the day. The only thing you can set include your meals.

Making a plan for your schedule is something that is very individual as each family is distinct with different hobbies and activities, schedules for work as well as family requirements. It can require some time to figure out an ideal schedule for you and your family.

Planning Your Homeschool

The process of planning your homeschooling year isn't easy. Based on the person you are and your preferred way of teaching There are a variety of methods to go about this.

As an example, kids who don't attend school don't like planning since they let their kids to determine what they'll study and how long. Even a tiny amount of making plans ahead could be beneficial.

Year Overview

It is recommended to start by reviewing your year. The big picture is what you should be looking at. Plan out your holiday breaks, days off, and break times on vacation that you're aware of prior to the time. Planning to go on vacation? Note the date down. Do you have a child? Make plans to take a long vacation right after your due. Make sure you include any birthdays or other special occasions.

You have the chance to imagine. Consider what your ideal homeschool could look like, how your children want to study, and where it would be possible to have breaks, go on holidays or conduct an entire unit of research. Spend some time dreaming about your ideal homeschool, then make a list for the year ahead. It's not going to be perfect however it will give you a rough outline as well as a sketch of what's in store for the year coming.

Popular Homeschool Ideas

Morning Basket

A breakfast basket is an ideal method to begin the day. It is easy to make and are completely adjustable. You basically have an empty basket, and put in a range of easy and enjoyable things to do. Brainteasers, flashcards, stories as well as puzzles are all common choices for your breakfast basket. They are straightforward items that youngsters can begin by themselves, and then Mom is finishing her coffee and then cleans up after breakfast. It's an excellent idea to get started in the morning easily and quickly.

Poetry Teatime

The time for poetry tea is where you sit around a table, prepare a cup of tea and enjoy an indulgence while reading the poetry. The older children may choose poems to read, while children younger than them can be told to read, or could choose from an Anthology. This is an excellent opportunity to spend time reading and with the family. We are awestruck by our poetry tea time! We sometimes choose the theme, or tailor it according to the time of year. It's a simple affair: we set the tablecloth out and light candles. We play classical music, enjoy cookies, drink a cup of tea (or juice) or read some poetry.